early years
training &
management

Gaining your NVQ Level 3 in Early Years Care and Education

10

Meg Jones

Editor	Author	Illustrations
Sarah Sodhi	Meg Jones	Adrian Barclay/Beehive Illustration
Assistant Editor	**Series Designer**	**Cover photograph**
Victoria Lee	Mark Udall	© Martyn Chillmaid
	Designer	
	Catherine Mason	

Acknowledgement

Her Majesty's Stationery Office and Queen's Printer for Scotland for the use of materials from *NVQ in Early Years Care and Education* produced by the Care Sector Consortium with funding from the Department for Education and Employment © 2000, Crown copyright.

Every effort has been made to trace copyright holders and the publishers apologise for any inadvertent omissions.

Text © 2003 Meg Jones
© 2003 Scholastic Ltd

Designed using Adobe PageMaker

Published by Scholastic Ltd, Villiers House, Clarendon Avenue, Leamington Spa, Warwickshire CV32 5PR

Visit our website at www.scholastic.co.uk

Printed by Bell & Bain Ltd, Glasgow

3 4 5 6 7 8 9 0   5 6 7 8 9 0 1 2

Gaining your NVQ Level 3 in Early Years Care and Education   **early years training & management**

Contents

Contents

Introduction

Taking an NVQ can be a daunting experience until you become familiar with the system and used to the language. However, it is a very practical way to gain a nationally recognised qualification that you can complete in your regular work setting. An NVQ Level 3 in Early Years Care and Education qualifies you to work in an unsupervised position with children up to the age of 8 years, in a range of settings.

You will need to prepare yourself for the practical aspects, demonstrate your understanding and knowledge of childcare and early years, and provide evidence of your work in a portfolio (a file), to the satisfaction of your assessor. The outcome is a qualification comparable to other recognised courses for unsupervised positions with young children. This book will help you to collect the evidence for the practical aspects you will need to undertake.

Following registration with an NVQ assessment centre you will be given a candidates copy of the *Guidance* and the *National Occupational Standards for Early Years Care and Education Level 3*. These detail the areas you need to cover, which are the same for all the awarding bodies. You will also be allocated an assessor, who will observe you at your work setting to ensure you are meeting the Standards. Working towards an NVQ is a two-way process between you and your assessor, who will have an early years background. Your assessor will explain what is required, help you to understand the terminology and guide you through the process. However, you have to do the work!

The Unit approach

An NVQ is presented in Units. A Level 3 qualification consists of 11 mandatory Units, plus three optional Units from a choice of 15. Throughout the process the NVQ is broken down into detail, to ensure everything is covered. Each Unit consists of a number of Elements addressing different aspects. Each Element presents a range of situations and the performance criteria that need to be demonstrated, either in the direct work with the children or by some other form, in order to meet the Standards. You can work your way through each Unit, but as life and learning does not come in neat categories, evidence presented for one Unit should be cross-referenced to others. Although this appears complicated and will take you some time to fully understand how it works, you can be assured that you will eventually grasp the concept. Remember you are not on your own, your assessor will help you.

This book suggests ideas and activities for each of the mandatory Units, on an Element-by-Element basis, plus four of the most popular optional Units.

Mandatory Units

C2 Provide for children's physical needs.
C3 Promote the physical development of children.
C5 Promote children's social and emotional development.
C7 Provide a framework for the management of behaviour.
C10 Promote children's sensory and intellectual development.

C11 Promote children's language and communication development.
C15 Contribute to the protection of children from abuse.
C16 Observe and assess the development and behaviour of children.
E3 Plan and equip environments for children.
M7 Plan, implement and evaluate learning activities and experiences.
P2 Establish and maintain relationships with parents.

Optional Units covered in this book

C14 Care for and promote the development of babies.
C17 Promote the care and education of children with special needs.
C24 Support the development of children's literacy skills.
C25 Support the development of children's mathematical skills.

Within your Standards

➤ You will see the titles listed above, these are the **Units**.
➤ Under each heading are between two and six sub-headings, these are the **Elements**.
➤ In each Element there are up to 11 **performance criteria**, referred to as PCs. These are the factors you have to demonstrate to prove your capability to work at the required standard.
➤ In a box by the performance criteria are the **range** statements. The range may cover children with and without difficulties, with and without special needs, indoors and outdoors, different methods, types of play, concepts and so on. It is identified, within each Unit, those areas that must be directly observed by your assessor, those that may be observed by a witness and those that you have to provide evidence for.
➤ Numbers and letters provide **quick references** to Units, Elements, and performance criteria. For example C2 'Provide for children's physical needs' is often referred to just as C2. The first Element in C2 is 'Plan, prepare and provide food and drink for children', so this is referred to as C2.1. The fourth performance criteria for this area is 'Learning situations that arise and can be created whilst preparing and serving food are appropriately used', and this is referred to as C2.1: 4.

➤ The **evidence** is the record of *direct observations* of you working with the children and *witness testimonies* signed by your colleagues when the assessor is not there. *Work products* can include copies of children's records, menus, charts, forms from your setting, letters and information to parents and carers, and examples of the children's work. *Child observations* and *reflective accounts* are your own accounts of what happened, how you dealt with it and an evaluation. Always ensure that children cannot be identified from any records you use in your portfolio. In addition, your supporting evidence can include *curriculum plans*, an *inspection* report of the setting, *diaries*, *log books* and *notes* recording everyday incidents, *case studies*, *assignments* and *simulations*, for example, when you are unable to get evidence for an emergency evacuation or a sick child. You can also be *questioned*, this can be both written and spoken (although both need to be recorded in writing for the portfolio). Any training you undertake, during an NVQ or a *prior achievement*, such as first aid or food hygiene, can be included. It must be recent; you must provide a certificate or letter of confirmation and a copy of the syllabus; and your assessor will question you on the relevant aspects. Your assessment centre will provide further details about this.

➤ You will need to demonstrate **knowledge and understanding** of what you are doing with the children. You can do this through your actions, questioning by your assessor, assignments and case studies. There is a page at the end of each Unit indicating what you need to know. You will be expected to attend training to underpin knowledge, read books and childcare magazines, and undertake your own research as required. Copies of magazine articles, policies prepared by others and photocopies of handouts are not evidence, but you can be questioned on them, which is evidence.

➤ The **setting** is a generic word used to mean any place of work with young children, where you will be assessed.

➤ Your assessor will work with you to produce **assessment plans** as an ongoing record of your progress. These also need to be included in your portfolio.

➤ Although you will probably work through the Units one or two at a time, it is preferable to take a **holistic** view. This means addressing more than one aspect at the same time. Life does not come in neat categories. If the children are playing in the home corner they will be communicating, developing self-esteem, reflecting their culture, developing fine motor skills, and displaying positive or unwanted behaviour. You will be interacting, communicating, aware of safety issues and reinforcing positive behaviour. This is a holistic approach.

➤ The **curriculum** refers to the range of activities and experiences offered to the children. To be effective you need to plan the activity, detail what the children will gain from it and evaluate it afterwards. There is also a place in the curriculum for unplanned opportunities.

➤ You will come across the term **cross-reference** in any NVQ documentation. This means that even though you may have planned an activity for one area, such as C3.1 'Develop children's confidence in movement', your assessor will also note how you deal with other areas, such as positive and negative behaviour (C7.2, C7.3), reinforcing language development and introducing new words (C11.2, C11.4, C11.5). You will be expected to plan the activity (M7.1, M7.3) and evaluate it afterwards (M7.4). So one activity will produce evidence for a number of Units. You need to assess each piece of evidence in your portfolio to see where it can be cross-referenced. It takes time to do this, as you need to know what is in the Standards, but your assessor will help you.

➤ In addition to the performance criteria identified in each Unit you are expected to conform to the **principles of good practice**. These are described in the NVQ Guidance and below.

➤ Your assessor will directly observe your practice to ensure you are carrying out the requirements with competence. If there are gaps in your knowledge or you need more practice, your assessor will suggest ways to gain the necessary evidence.

➤ Your assessor will give you regular **feedback** on your progress.

➤ You need to provide at least **three** different types of evidence in each Unit. When you meet the Standards your assessor will sign your work off and declare that competence has been met.

➤ Make sure all the evidence you have produced has your **signature** on it to confirm it is your own work. Your assessor will also sign and date it.

➤ Once a Unit is completed it is submitted to the assessment centre for **internal verification**. A trained verifier, who knows the Standards well and who may also be an assessor, checks that all the necessary documentation is in place and that there is sufficient, reliable and recent evidence in your portfolio to judge your competence.

The principles of good practice

These statements are based on the current legislation and guidance, including the United Nations Convention on the Rights of the Child, the Children Act 1989, relevant curricula and accepted good practice. Strands of the principles should permeate throughout the NVQ. The relevant principles are listed at the front of each Unit. These must be put into practice for you to meet the requirements of the NVQ.

1 The welfare of the child

All practical work with children should give a high priority to their welfare. Children have a right to quality care in a safe environment, to be treated with respect by caring adults, to be listened to and to be protected from harm. Children must never be shaken, smacked, slapped or ridiculed. Demonstrate that children are the focus of your thinking in your work and portfolio.

2 Keeping children safe

Children need protecting from the environment and abuse by adults. You must be aware of the safety implications when children are taking part in activities and at all other times. For example, when planning outdoor play, do a risk assessment on the area, the equipment, supervision and potential hazards. Children should be kept safe and their health protected; this includes accurate record-keeping and emergency procedures.

3 Working in partnership with parents/families

You need to recognise that parents and carers are children's first educators. Together practitioners and parents can offer the best developmental support for children, by sharing information. Respect must be given to children from different backgrounds and traditions, and parents' wishes taken into consideration. Record the children's developmental progress and share with the parents.

4 Children's learning and development

The majority of activities offered in an under-eights setting can be used as a learning experience. Children should be offered a wide range of experiences and activities, including physical, intellectual, emotional, social, communication and spiritual. For example, when you plan for water play consider the gross motor skills of lifting and pouring, the mathematical concepts of volume and measurement, the scientific aspects of floating and sinking, the emotional benefit of self-reliance and satisfaction, the behaviour management of not splashing others and communication through interaction with peers. Have learning objectives for each lesson or activity plan and evaluate it afterwards.

5 Equality of opportunity
Every child should have an equal chance of accessing all opportunities for learning and development. The aim is for all children to reach their full potential and that means treating each child as an individual. Avoid stereotyping and consider the cultural implications of each activity you organise. Look at your plans critically. Do they exclude children with special needs? How could you adapt them to be inclusive? Widen your knowledge by studying the impact of disability and the cultural backgrounds of all the children. Equality of opportunity extends to cover family members and colleagues.

6 Anti-discrimination
Every person working in early years care and education must ensure that no one is discriminated against on the grounds of gender, racial origins, religion, culture, social background, disability, class, family unit or sexual orientation. Consider how you would challenge discriminatory language between children.

7 Celebrating diversity
We live in a multicultural, multilingual, multifaith, multiracial society. This should be reflected in your work regardless of whether you have children from minority ethnic groups in your setting or children for whom English is an additional language. Consider whether your setting visually reflects cultural diversity. Children need to develop a sense of identity within their cultural background and to learn about cultures different to their own. We all have a culture and this should be respected.

8 Confidentiality
Every setting should have a policy on confidentiality. Never discuss information about children, families or colleagues outside work. Find out about the confidentiality policy in your

setting. Do not present evidence in your portfolio that can be used to identify children. Use a fictitious name or code, or simply omit the name. If you use a fictitious name, make this clear on the document so the assessors and verifiers know it is not genuine.

9 Working with other professionals

Always remember you are not working alone. When unsure, and where appropriate, seek advice from others who are more experienced than yourself. Working as part of a team is a vital element in quality childcare. Respect other professionals. Be a good team-worker.

10 The reflective practitioner

Be prepared to look back over your work, seek advice from your supervisor, accept further training and develop your skills throughout your period of work with the children and their families.

Using the book

This book is designed to offer a range of activities and ideas to cover all the practical aspects of the NVQ in Early Years Care and Education Level 3. It does not include underpinning knowledge that would need to be gained from other sources.

There is a main activity for each Element, a case study, questions, tips, a 'Did you know?' slot and extra ideas. Indications are given as to which range statement or performance criteria may be met, but this is not exclusive. When you complete activities sometimes you will cover them all, other times you will miss some out. Your assessor may identify further ones not stated here. Every candidate will operate differently. At the end of each Unit there are 'answer pointers', which are key words in random order. They are not intended to be everything you can say about a subject, but just enough to get you started. It is intended that the answers should be written out in full.

At the end of the book are a number of photocopiable sheets. These are included to help you in the process of gaining your NVQ. There are back-up pages to support suggested activities and sample forms for recording plans, observations and children's development. NVQs require a flexible approach, there are no set forms, so you may choose to use the forms used by your setting or the ones included here. It is important that you use planning sheets to show you have thought through the whole planning process, you offer a balanced curriculum, the learning objectives have been identified, the preparation required has been thought through and you have evaluated activities offered.

You will not need to do everything in this book to gain the qualification. By taking a holistic approach, one activity could cover a number of different Units and Elements. If you plan carefully to incorporate as much variety as possible, during one direct observation, you can be very time efficient. This book will give you choice.

Gaining an NVQ is not the easy option and it does not suit everyone. There is a lot of work to be done, a mass of paperwork to be organised and a whole new language to learn. By the end of the NVQ you will have covered every aspect of early years care and education, will have honed your skills, and learned a great deal. This is just the start – good luck!

C2 Provide for children's physical needs

This Unit covers the physical care of the children as part of the regular routine. At the heart of the Unit is the welfare of the child, carrying out care in a safe and competent manner, ensuring that you understand and consider parents and carers' wishes.

This Unit will enable you to:
C2.1 Plan, prepare and provide food and drink for children
C2.2 Contribute to children's personal hygiene
C2.3 Respond to illness in children
C2.4 Plan and provide quiet periods for children.

Element C2.1 Plan, prepare and provide food and drink for children

➤ Your assessor can observe and question you. · **C2.1**: range 1b, c ◄

Flower bonnets
Number of children: six.

Resources
Plain round biscuits; marshmallows; icing flower cake decorations; icing sugar; water; shallow containers; blunt knives; beakers; aprons; jug of milk.

Preparation
Plan the activity using the 'Activity plan' photocopiable sheet on page 131. Check for any food allergies or dietary requirements. Clean the table surfaces. Ask all the children and adults to put on clean aprons and wash their hands. Mix the icing sugar with water to a spreadable paste in the shallow dishes.

What to do
➤ Ensure that each child has a biscuit, a dish of icing paste and a beaker.
➤ Invite the children to spread a thin layer of icing sugar over their biscuits.
➤ Encourage the children to place a marshmallow in the centre and to add a ring of icing flowers around the edge of the biscuit to create a hat rim.
➤ Let one child serve the others with milk as they all eat their 'bonnets'.

> ✔ **Tip**
>
> ➤ Take a Basic Food Hygiene course at your local college or through the Local Authority Environmental Health Department.
>
> **C2.1**: 3

Support and extension

Show younger children what to do and let them decorate their 'bonnets' in their own way. Encourage older children to use coloured icing to make patterns.

Evaluation

➤ *Cross-reference to **M7***   Evaluate the session. What worked or was unsatisfactory? What will you ◄ change if you do it again? How can you develop it? Did any children experience difficulties? How can individual children be assisted with certain tasks? Record your plan for the activity, take photos and include your evaluation.

Supporting activity

➤ **C2.2**: *4 range 2b,* · · Use a health promotion poster to show the children how to wash hands ◄
*cross-reference **C10**,*   correctly using soap and a nailbrush. Let the children practise.
C5

Case study

Nina's family are vegans, with strict food preparation requirements. They are anxious the setting cannot accommodate Nina's cultural needs. How can you reassure them and what foods can you provide? Write down the case study with your responses for your portfolio.

Follow on

➤ **C2.1**: *1, 2* · · · · · ·   Familiarise yourself with the dietary requirements of a range of different ◄ backgrounds and cultures. Find out about social aspects associated with preparation, food and eating. Be aware of the different eating and drinking utensils available and when using hands to eat is acceptable, including for different ages and abilities. Talk to parents and carers about their preferences and experiences.

Questions

(See answer pointers at end of chapter.)

➤ **C2.1**: *6* · · · · · · · · ·   **1.** *Should all children use a knife and fork by the age of four years? Explain.* ◄
➤ **C2.1**: *7* · · · · · · · · ·   **2.** *How can the eating environment ensure the physical comfort of children?* ◄
➤ **C2.1**: *8* · · · · · · · · ·   **3.** *Describe the social skills acquired while eating and drinking together.* ◄

Record the questions and your answers and share these with your assessor.

Did you know?

Food allergies occur when the immune system reacts to food or additives. Food intolerance is similar, but does not affect the immune system.

C2.1: *1, 5*

Extra ideas

➤ **C2.1**: *1* · · · · · · · ·   Draw up a weekly menu sheet suitable for three- to five-year-olds, using the ◄ photocopiable sheet on page 156.
➤ **C2.1**: *1* · · · · · · · ·   Plan an alternative weekly menu sheet for vegetarian children. ◄

Element C2.2 Contribute to children's personal hygiene

➤ Your assessor can observe and question you. · · · · · · · · · · · · · · · · **C2.2**: *range 2d* ◄

Smile please
Number of children: small group.

Resources
Skin tone card; thin white card; A4 backing paper; hair-coloured crêpe paper; thick cardboard; magazine pictures of smiling faces; scissors; glue; pencils; toothbrushes and toothpaste.

Preparation
Plan the activity using the 'Activity plan' photocopiable sheet on page 131. For each child, cut out a circle of skin tone card, approximately 15cm in diameter. Cut the crêpe paper into strips.

What to do
➤ Cut out smiling faces and glue around the edge of the backing paper.
➤ On a card circle draw a smiley face with a prominent mouth in the centre.
➤ Invite the children to glue the crêpe 'hair' in place, suggesting different styles, such as long, short, curly, straight, plaited, bunched and fringed.
➤ Cut out rows of shiny white teeth and glue them into the mouth.
➤ Let the children fold the cardboard into four, flatten it and glue to the centre of the paper. Glue the face to the cardboard to give it a 3-D effect.
➤ Ask the children to write their names on card and glue to the paper.
➤ Discuss cleaning teeth and let them practise with their toothbrushes.

✔ Tip
➤ Apples soften tooth enamel; do not clean teeth until at least half an hour after eating apples.

C2.2: 4

Support and extension
Give younger children pre-cut pictures and teeth, and scribe their names for them. Enlarge the 'Reward chart' photocopiable sheet (page 138) to A3 size. Display when older children have cleaned their teeth using stars in the squares.

Evaluation
➤ What worked and what was unsatisfactory. What will you change? How can . . you develop the activity? Think about any difficulties that individual children experienced. How can individual children be assisted with certain activities or tasks? In what ways can you promote personal hygiene?

Cross-reference to **M7** ◄

Supporting activity
➤ Create a set of matching cards, one half with a picture, the other half with an appropriate phrase. For example, 'I brush my hair in the morning' with a picture of a hairbrush. Each player turns a card in turn to find a matching pair.

Cross-reference to ◄
C.24, C.10

Case study

Liam, aged four, has been dry since he was two-and-a-half. You find him in the home corner, wet and distressed. This has happened several times recently. How will you deal with the situation? What could the reasons be? Write down the case study with your responses for your portfolio.

Follow on

➤ **C2.2**: 3, 8 . . . . Identify ways to help children in their toileting, encouraging confidence, self-reliance, self-esteem and asking adults for help when appropriate. ◄

Questions

(See answer pointers at end of chapter.)

➤ **C2.2**: 3 . . . . **4.** *Describe how waste products and soiled items are disposed of in your setting.* ◄

➤ **C2.2**: 5 . . . . **5.** *How would you care for an African-Caribbean child's tightly curled hair?* ◄

➤ **C2.2**: 8 . . . . **6.** *How would you deal with a toilet training accident so as not to undermine the child's self-esteem?* ◄

Record the questions and your answers and share these with your assessor.

Did you know?

African-Caribbean children may have dry skin; parents may want to put baby oil on it. Remember dark skin can burn in the sun so keep children covered and use sun lotion.

C2.2: 5

Extra idea

➤ **C2.2**: 10, cross- · · · Place appropriate number cards on the toilet doors. Count the numbers with ◄
reference to **C24**   the children. Ask the children to choose a number when using the toilet.

Element C2.3 Respond to illness in children

➤ **C2.3**: 1, cross- · · · · Your assessor can observe and question you. ◄
reference to **C10**

Hospital corner

Number of children: four.

Resources

Small bed or mattress; blanket; low table; chairs; selection of bandages and slings; toy medicine bottles and spoons; screen; dolls and cots; clipboard; paper; pencils; nurses and doctors outfits; medical and surgical instruments; tissues; healthy eating posters.

Preparation

Plan using the 'Activity plan' photocopiable sheet (page 131). Set out the role-play area as a hospital, using signs such as 'Wait here' and 'Ward 6'.

What to do

➤ Talk with the children about the different roles.
➤ Encourage the children to talk about their own experiences of illness.
➤ Explain that children must tell adults if something hurts.
➤ Introduce new words, such as 'medicine', 'patient' and 'emergency'.
➤ Discuss healthy eating, exercise, rest and looking after your body.
➤ Reassure any children who may be worried about illness and hospitals.
➤ Encourage the children to role-play being patients or medical personnel.
➤ Help children write notes or make marks using the clipboard, paper and pen.

Support and extension

If a child becomes distressed, comfort them and suggest an activity, such as making the doll better. Extend the discussion with older children to include paramedics, physiotherapists, pharmacists and X-rays.

Evaluation

What did the children think about the activity? Did they like role-playing hospitals? What did they like best? How else could the area be set up? What are the children gaining from role-play? How can individual children be helped?

Supporting activity

Invite medical personnel, such as a nurse in uniform or a doctor with a stethoscope and bag, into the setting so they can discuss their jobs with the children.

Case study

Asha is 15 months old. She starts crying and touching her ear. She is obviously unwell, but cannot tell you how. What could the cause be and what action will you take? Write down the case study with your responses for your portfolio.

Follow on

➤ Familiarise yourself with signs and symptoms of common childhood illness. Consider how to identify signs in a child who cannot communicate. Be aware of when you should contact the parents and seek medical help.

C2.3: 1, 2, 3, 4, 10 ◄

Questions

(See answer pointers at end of chapter.)
➤ 7. *What are the signs and symptoms to alert you to illness in a young child?* · · **C2.3**: 1 ◄
➤ 8. *When would you seek medical advice for a child?* · · · · · · · · · · · · · **C2.3**: 3 ◄
➤ 9. *In the event of acute illness or accident what do you need to assess, in what* · **C2.3**: 1, 3 ◄
order and what action should you take?

Record the questions and your answers and share these with your assessor.

 Tip

➤ Ensure that other members of staff are aware that you need to be observed caring for sick children. Ask staff to call on you, if practical, to deal with a situation if it arises while your assessor is present.

C2. 3: range 1a, b, 2a, b, c

➤ Show your assessor actual completed paperwork from your setting, including written instruction from parents on administering prescribed medication. Also show records of administered medication. Your assessor may question you on this.

C2.3: 5, 7

➤ You need to know where and how medication is stored in your setting. Show your assessor the relevant cupboards and refrigerators, the medication and the legibility of the labels.

C2.3: 6

C2.3: 1, 3

Did you know?

Vomiting is not necessarily caused by problems in the stomach. It can occur due to generalised infection, common infectious diseases, feeding problems or psychological disturbances. If the child is also drowsy, medical opinion should always be sought.

Extra idea

> ➤ Cross-reference to · · ·
> **C5**

Give the children simple lessons in first aid. Provide a bowl of water, cotton ◄ wool, bandages and slings.

Element C2.4 Plan and provide quiet periods for children

> ➤ **C2.4: range** 1c · · · ·

Your assessor can observe and question you. ◄

Friendship bracelets

Number of children: four.

Resources

Thin ribbon; coloured threads; metallic threads, if possible; cereal box cardboard; cardboard packet, such as a tea packet; sticky tape.

> ✔ **Tip**
>
> ➤ Be aware of the importance of comforters to the child.
>
> **C2.4**: 6
>
> ➤ Consider safety aspects when using small items, appropriate to the age of the children.
>
> **C2**.4: 2

Preparation

Plan the activity using the 'Activity plan' photocopiable sheet on page 131. Cut one side of the cereal box into a large Y shape with 'arms' 15cm apart. Cut a slit in the cardboard packet, to hold the 'leg' of the Y. Use sticky tape to fix the Y upright. Cut 30cm of ribbon. Cut several 40cm lengths of thread.

What to do

➤ Place the ribbon flat on the table. Lay three or four threads along the ribbon, with all the ends at one end together (so the threads at the other end are 10cm longer than the ribbon).
➤ Tie the parallel ends together with a knot, leaving 5cm at the end to tie.
➤ Tape the knot on to the top of one 'arm' of the Y.
➤ Stretch the ribbon across the Y, so it is not loose, and tape to the other 'arm' (threads should dangle from the knot).
➤ Wind the threads, one at a time, around the ribbon.
➤ When they are all collected at the opposite 'arm', pull the sticky tape off and knot the opposite end, leaving 5cm for tying.
➤ Encourage the children to give their bracelet to a friend.
➤ Talk about making things for others, friendship and being kind.

Support and extension

You can help younger children assemble the bracelet. They can wind the threads around the ribbon. Older children will be able to wind individual threads to make certain patterns, or more elaborate plaited, woven or twisted bracelets.

Evaluation

➤ Is this an effective quiet activity? What worked and what was unsatisfactory?   *Cross-reference to* **C3** ◄
What will you change if you do it again? How can you make the activity more
varied depending on the developmental level of the children? Note any
difficulties that individual children experienced.

Supporting activity

Find out about the festival of Raksha Bandhan. This Hindu festival, held in
August, is when sisters make or buy twisted thread bands, often red and
golden, but they can be any colour, to tie around their brother's wrists. The
braid is called a rakhi, which means protection. Tying a rakhi is a symbolic
binding of brothers and sisters. The brother will often give a gift of flowers,
sweets, money or clothes to his sister. A Raksha Bandhan card can be given.

Case study

Two-year-old Jessica is to start at your nursery the following week. In
discussion with the parents you discover Jessica has a ragged piece of
cloth as a comforter. They are anxious not to upset Jessica, as this will be
the first time she has left them. What advice will you give the parents?
How will you deal with the situation in the nursery? Write down the case
study with your responses for your portfolio.

Follow on

➤ Over a period of time record all the different comfort objects children   **C2.4**: 6   ◄
bring into the nursery with them. Add to the list any others that parents
may have told you about, or you have seen while out in the community.
Consider how you can ensure these objects can be kept clean and
hygienic. Write down your findings.

Questions

(See answer pointers at end of chapter.)
➤ **10.** *What quiet activities would you plan into the routine?* · · · · · · · · · **C2.4**: 1   ◄
➤ **11.** *What rituals and settling routines would you expect to find in your setting?*   **C 2.4**: 7   ◄
➤ **12.** *Describe how you would wake up a sleeping child.* · · · · · · · · · · · · · · **C2.4**: 10   ◄

Record the questions and your answers and share these with your assessor.

Did you know?

Physical changes take place during sleep: heart rate slows; pupils
contract; brain waves change; digestive juice, saliva and urine
production slows down; breathing and the intake of oxygen diminishes.
All this in addition to losing consciousness.

C2.4: 1

Extra ideas

➤ Use buttons for quiet activities, ensuring that children are carefully supervised   **C2. 4**: *range 1c*   ◄
at all times. Find out if there is a waste recycling centre or a garment factory
in the area – bags of buttons may be available from them.

Use buttons for:
- Counting
- Sticking to pictures or models as eyes or wheels
- Counters in games
- Use with play dough
- Covering small 'treasure' boxes
- Threading
- Collages.

Practical ways of collecting evidence

> **C2.4**: *1, range 1a,*
> *b, c*

Keep a diary for a week noting all the opportunities children have to rest. Record the time of day, the length of time they rest, whether they sleep or have quiet activities and the type of activity. Show how information is passed on to parents and carers. Evaluate current practices. Can they be improved?

Check your progress
To complete the Unit ensure that you have been observed by your assessor for at least one aspect of each range statement. If you do not normally prepare meals, incorporate food preparation or cooking into an activity at your setting. Your assessor can observe different aspects of toileting and personal hygiene on more than one occasion. Dealing with sick and injured children cannot be planned in advance, so arrange with your colleagues that when your assessor is present you will deal with minor injuries and illness. At other times you will need to organise a witness testimony. You will need to show your assessor how you offer the balance of active and quiet activities.

Answer pointers
Ensure your answers are fully made for your assessor.
1. No. Cultural alternatives. Physical impairment. Lack of practice.
2. Clean. Correct height tables and chairs. Distraction-free. Noise levels.
3. Socially-acceptable patterns. Use of implements. Try new things. Language.
4. Safety. Hygiene. Yellow bags. Sealed nappy bins. Sealed plastic bags.
5. Check with parents. Wide-toothed comb. Conditioner.
6. Sensitive. Matter-of-fact. Discrete. Independent.
7. Skin/temperature change. Diarrhoea. Vomit. Drowsy. Lack hunger. Irritable.
8. Severity of symptoms. Check setting procedures.
9. Recognise. Report. Reassure. Medical attention. Children away. 999. Parents.
10. Drawing. Reading. Jigsaws. Talking quietly. Small craft activities.
11. Toileting. Closing curtains. Drink. Comforters. Story. Cuddles.
12. Speaking quietly. Unhurried. Sympathetically. Stroking.

Further information
Early Years Care and Education by Penny Tassoni and Kath Bulman
(Heinemann Child Care, 1999)

C3 Promote the physical development of children

This Unit covers the promotion of children's physical development. It emphasises the importance of freedom of expression and the development of both gross and fine motor skills.

This chapter will enable you to:
C3.1 Develop children's confidence in movement
C3.2 Develop children's skills of locomotion and balance
C3.3 Develop children's gross motor skills
C3.4 Develop children's fine motor skills.

Element C3.1 Develop children's confidence in movement

➤ Your assessor can observe and question you. · ◀ *C3.1: range 1b, 2a, b, 3a*

Let's dance
Number of children: eight.

Resources
Ribbons or strips of crêpe paper; ankle bells; hoops; floaty fabrics, such as sari material; masks; tinsel; storage box; tape or CD player; assorted music tapes or CDs with a range of tempo, strong beats, familiar and unfamiliar.

Preparation
Plan the activity using the 'Activity plan' photocopiable sheet on page 131. Clear a large space and place the resources in a box in the centre.

What to do
➤ Explain the session to the children and ask them to listen carefully.
➤ Play the music and encourage the children to imagine how to dance to it.
➤ Ask the children to find a space and lead with warming-up exercises.
➤ Invite the children to dance with props to short pieces of music.
➤ Allow the children to experiment with moving at their own pace.
➤ Finish the session with gentle winding-down exercises.

Support and extension
➤ Suggest props and movements for younger children. Devise a simple routine for older children to follow, such as run, stamp, twirl, wave and gallop.

 Tip
➤ Use a variety of learning aids to support the expression of movement, such as musical instruments, tapes and CDs, recorded birdsong and the human voice.

C3.1: 5 ◀

Cross-reference to ◀
C11

Evaluation

Review the dancing with the children. Which music did they like best and why? What other props can be used? Discuss your thoughts about the session with your assessor. Would you repeat it? Would you make changes? If so, how and why? Explain why you need to warm up and wind down.

Supporting activities

➤ *Cross-reference to · · · · Devise further activities based on dancing, such as 'dance' out a story, put on ◄
C10 a show, set up the role-play area as a theatre; make a display of dancers from different cultures; invite a local dance class to the setting.

➤ **C3.1**: 1 · · · · · · · ·

Case study

Dillon loves music, but his mobility difficulties make it hard to dance. How ◄ can you ensure he can participate in music and movement sessions? Write down the case study with your responses for your portfolio.

➤ **C3.1**: 6 · · · · · · · ·

Follow on

Considering a range of disabilities, suggest how to give all children an ◄ inclusive experience and help them gain confidence in movement. Ideas include wheeled toys, climbing, balancing, jumping and action songs.

Questions

(See answer pointers at end of chapter.)

➤ **C3.1**: 1 · · · · · · · · · **1.** *List activities and equipment for different ages to develop movement.* ◄
➤ **C3.1**: 3 · · · · · · · · · **2.** *Suggest ways to raise children's awareness of their own bodies.* ◄
➤ **C3.1**: 6 · · · · · · · · **3.** *How can you ensure physical activities do not reinforce stereotypes?* ◄

Record the questions and your answers and share these with your assessor.

Did you know?

The most valuable and accessible instrument and learning aid that we have is the human voice. Use it to express the different qualities of movement (slow, gentle, forceful) and for onomatopoeic words (words sounding like the sounds they describe, such as splash, hiss and whiz).

C3.1: 5

Extra idea

➤ **C3.1**: 1, 2, 3, 4, 5, · · · Using simple card headbands with rabbit ears, frog eyes or crocodile mouth ◄
6, *cross-reference* attached, ask the children to act out their animal's movements.
to **C24**

Element C3.2 Develop children's skills of locomotion and balance

➤ **C3.2**: *range 1b,* · · · · Your assessor can observe and question you. ◄
2a, b, 3b

Going on a journey

Number of children: four.

Resources
Open space, outdoors if possible; large sheet of paper; thick felt pens; chalk or washing lines; hoops; stepping-stones; PE cones; dressing-up clothes; backpacks; 'treasure chest' containing a surprise; sand-coloured cloth.

Preparation
Plan the activity using the 'Activity plan' photocopiable sheet on page 131. Check that the open space is hazard free.

What to do
➤ Ask the children to draw a treasure map on a large sheet of paper. Suggest they draw an island with mountains, beaches, palm trees, rocks and a stream. Draw a path around the island leading to the treasure.

➤ Working co-operatively, chalk a large outline of the island on the playground surface or arrange the washing lines to form the outline.

➤ As a group, arrange the equipment on the 'island' following the map as a guide. Fixed outdoor equipment can be incorporated, so a climbing frame can be a mountain. Hide the treasure chest under the cloth at the end of the trail.

➤ Invite the children to wear their backpacks and become explorers. Play 'Follow-the-leader', encouraging the children to balance on stepping-stones, weave around cones and put on disguises, as they follow the path.

➤ Celebrate when the children 'find' the treasure.

Support and extension
Help younger children draw the map. Keep the activities simple and guide them when necessary. Challenge older children to draw individual maps.

Evaluation
Was the activity at the appropriate level for the children? Did they practise their balance and locomotion? How did the activity encourage co-operative play? Did each child play the leader? Was it fun?

Supporting activity
➤ Talk to the children about locomotion. Show the children pictures of people in different poses and describe their movements. Glue the pictures to a large sheet of paper and attach the appropriate labels.

C3.2: 3 ◄

Case study
➤ Kate's grandma says she is unsteady, always bumps into things and falls over. How will you respond? What can you do to establish the current level of development? Who will you inform and what action can they take? Write down the case study with your responses for your portfolio.

C3.2: 1 ◄

Follow on
➤ Find out about the normal behaviour for this age group. Discuss this with your assessor. Research conditions that can affect balance and locomotion, including inner ear infections, cerebral palsy and dyspraxia.

Cross-reference to ◄
C17

✔ Tip
➤ Check that all equipment is safe before allowing children to use it.

C3.2: 6 cross-reference to E3

➤ Encourage all children to take the leadership role when presenting activities.

C3.2: 5

➤ If you use a fictitious name in your evidence, ensure that this is recorded on the chart for the benefit of the internal and external verifiers.

Questions

(See answer pointers at end of chapter.)

➤ **C3.2**: 1 · · · · · · · · **4.** *How can fixed equipment be used to develop balance?* ◄

➤ **C3.2**: 4 · · · · · · · · **5.** *How can you encourage co-operative play relating to locomotion and balance?* ◄

➤ **C3.2**: 7 · · · · · · · · **6.** *Where can you find opportunities to develop the skills of locomotion and balance in the daily routine?* ◄

Record the questions and your answers and share these with your assessor.

Did you know?

Research shows that our physical make-up and actions are affected by our gender. However, culture also has a powerful influence on the way we raise children; boys and girls are brought up to be different. As practitioners we need to avoid stereotyping and to offer equality of opportunity in play and activities, to give children as wide an experience as possible.

C3.2: 5

Extra idea

➤ **C3.2**: 1 · · · · · · · · Use the 'I can:' photocopiable sheet on page 133 to plot a child's ◄
development. Observe real experiences and record gross motor skills, such as 'climb well' and 'throw a ball', or fine motor skills, such as 'dress myself' and 'use scissors'. Fill the sheet in with the child and send home as a home link.

Element C3.3 Develop children's gross motor skills

➤ **C3.3**: range 1a, c, · · · Your assessor can observe and question you. ◄
2a or b

PE activity

Number of children: whole group with assistance.

Resources

Large open space indoors or outside; large equipment such as climbing frame, balancing bars, benches, jumping boxes, crash mats; small equipment such as beanbags, bats, balls, skipping ropes, hoops and frisbees.

Preparation

Plan the activity using the 'Activity plan' photocopiable sheet on page 131. Arrange groups of large equipment to develop different gross motor skills. Different areas could involve walking on a balance beam followed by a jump, climbing and moving the body along a bar, and throwing beanbags into a hoop.

Ensure that the activities are appropriate to the age and development of the children, as inappropriate actions could cause injury.

What to do

➤ Introduce warm-up exercises to the children.

➤ Divide the children into small groups to be supervised by an adult.

➤ Carefully explain the movements expected of the children. Suggest that the children devise their own actions to link different movements.

➤ Allow the children as much freedom and decision-making as possible.

➤ Move the groups around so everyone has a turn on all the equipment.

➤ Praise and encourage the children for innovative movements, good teamwork, controlled actions and appropriate behaviour.

Support and extension

Use lower equipment, simpler routines and have more adults present with very young children. Present older children with more challenging equipment and complex routines. Ensure adults are ready to assist with all age groups.

Evaluation

Were the activities appropriate to the group of children? Note the children that easily achieved the planned activities and any that had difficulties. Record these on personal record sheets. How can you vary this activity? What other equipment can be introduced? How can you vary it only using small equipment? Can you plan a gross motor skills session without equipment? Make a note of your assessment and include in your portfolio.

Supporting activities

Discuss food, sleep and exercise. Make a display of healthy food from children's drawings. Set up the role-play area as a health food shop. Organise a simple aerobics session, taking care the children do not over stretch.

Case study

➤ Shaista's mother wears traditional Muslim dress, always keeping her body, arms, legs and head covered. She is anxious that her daughter does not expose her legs where male teachers and boys may be present. For school she always wears trousers underneath her school uniform. How will you respond to Shaista's mother and how can you resolve the situation for the PE session? Write down the case study with your responses for your portfolio.

C3.3: 8   ◄

Follow on

Find out about Muslim traditions and consider how you can accommodate them in your setting. How can you help the children understand different religious and cultural practices? Look at your setting's Equal Opportunities Policy. Does it address the needs you have identified in your studies? If not, discuss with your manager. Share your findings with your assessor.

Questions

(See answer pointers at end of chapter.)

➤ **7.** *How do you ensure safety in a physical activity session?* · · · · · · · · · · · · *C3.3*: 2, 3, 6, 7   ◄

Tip

➤ Raise children's awareness of the need for physical activity by discussing all the opportunities in the daily routine.

C3.3: 5

➤ **C3.3**: *4, 7* · · · · · · · **8.** *How can you ensure property is not damaged and the best use is made of* ◀
the available space?

➤ **C3.3**: *8* · · · · · · · · **9.** *What strategies can you use to encourage all children to participate?* ◀

Record the questions and your answers and share these with your assessor.

> **Did you know?**
> Children benefit more from regular exercise, such as a daily walk or
> running in the garden every day, rather than in short spurts, like a
> game of football or the occasional use of a climbing frame in the park.
> This is because it encourages a lifetime of good habits rather then
> irregular bursts of exercise.
>
> **C3.3**: *5, 8*

Extra idea

➤ **C3.3**: *5, 8* · · · · · · · During break time encourage children to play actively in the playground. ◀

Element C3.4 Develop children's fine motor skills

➤ **C3.4**: *range 1b, 2b* · · Your assessor can observe and question you. ◀

Design with mendhi
Number of children: four.

Resources
Skin tone paper; brown or orange felt pens; scissors; display board or large
sheet of coloured paper.

Preparation
Plan the activity using the 'Activity plan' photocopiable sheet on
page 131. Make copies of the 'Mendhi' photocopiable sheet on
page 134 for each child.

What to do
➤ Talk to the children about their hands. Name the parts, count
the fingers and discuss what you can wear on your hands, such as
gloves and rings.
➤ Show the children the 'Mendhi' sheet and discuss different ways
of decorating hands using rings, nail polish, nail decorations and
mendhi.
➤ Alternatively invite the children to draw around their own hands
onto sheets of paper and use these as a template.
➤ Encourage the children to practise drawing different rows of
small patterns and lines on plain paper; spotted, wavy and curved.
➤ Ask the children to decorate the paper hand using the brown or
orange felt pens. Finish by writing each child's name on the wrist of
the paper hand.

➤ Help the children to carefully cut around the hand.
➤ Create a mini display of all the hands on a display board.

Support and extension

Invite younger children to make their own marks on the paper hand and ensure an adult cuts out the hand. Encourage older children to make a series of elaborately decorated hands or matching left and right hands. Use these as a border for a display about Asian weddings, with photographs in the centre.

Evaluation

How appropriate was this activity for the age group? Did the children manage to draw and cut out shapes? Did they learn anything new? Did the activity stimulate discussion? Were any of the children more or less advanced in fine motor skills than you previously thought? Who will you inform, or where will you record this finding? Discuss with your assessor.

Supporting activities

Invite a member of the local community, who can demonstrate mendhi, into the setting. Cut out pictures of Asian brides showing their hands.

Tip
➤ Fixing the paper to a clipboard will prevent it slipping as younger children draw around their hands.
➤ Parents will not be pleased with a semi-permanent henna tattoo on their daughter's hand if she is to be a bridesmaid the following day. Always get parental permission first.

Case study

➤ Three-year-old Joe spends every weekday at the nursery and goes to bed when he gets home. At weekends he stays at his grandparents'. He does not have many opportunities to develop his fine motor skills at home. In what ways can you help Joe develop his hand–eye co-ordination and fine motor skills? Write down the case study with your responses for your portfolio.

C3.4: 3, 4 ◄

Follow on

➤ Using an early years resources catalogue select a range of toys and equipment suitable for developing fine motor skills. Cut them out and arrange as a montage inside a circle on an A4 sheet of paper. Around the outside edge list the type of activities available, such as matching games, jigsaws and painting. Place in your portfolio.

C3.4: 1 ◄

Questions

(See answer pointers at end of chapter.)
➤ **10.** *What activities promote hand–eye co-ordination?* · · · · · · · · · · **C3.4**: 4 ◄
➤ **11.** *Describe the opportunities to develop fine motor skills in the daily routine.* · · **C3.4**: 5 ◄
➤ **12.** *How can children be assisted and encouraged to use fine manipulation?* · · · **C3.4**: 7 ◄

Record the questions and yourl answers and share these with your assessor.

Did you know?

Young children are more likely to express their fears in drawings than by talking about them. If a child is involved in drawing they may talk to an adult when at other times they will not.

C3.4: 1

➤ **C3.4**: *1* · · · · · · · ·

Extra idea
Make a list of the equipment in your setting that gives opportunities for developing fine motor skills. ◄

Practical ways of collecting evidence

➤ **C3.1**: *1, cross-* · · · · ·
reference to **C16**

Observe the children in physically activities. Note when they are most active, ◄ what activities they enjoy and where they take place. Record the type of activity on a graph to assess the skills involved. Are the activities inclusive and how can they be improved? Review the procedures in the setting to see if more active play can be incorporated in the routine.

> ### Check your progress
> To complete the Unit ensure you have been observed by your assessor for at least one aspect of each range statement. If any of the performance criteria has not been observed you will need to use other types of evidence, which may include reflective accounts of your own performance and evaluation. If you do not normally set up physical activity sessions ask the person responsible if you can be involved in one. Take part in planning a session and be responsible for a group of children completing a range of activities.

Answers pointers
Ensure your answers are fully made for your assessor.
1. At two, four and seven years. Familiar movements. Wheeled toys.
2. Contact with equipment. Body movements. Descriptive words.
3. Girls and football. Wheeled vehicles. Skipping. Racial stereotypes.
4. Climbing frames. Tree trunks. See-saw. Painted lines. Balancing bars.
5. Pairing. Groups. Sharing equipment. Turn taking. Following.
6. Walking to setting. Vocabulary. Outdoor play. Activities.
7. Planning. Supervision. Room layout. Demonstration. Control.
8. Planning. Siting of equipment. Distance from vulnerable areas.
9. Equal opportunity. Not discriminate. Not stereotype. Aware of background.
10. Posting boxes. Jigsaws. Manipulative toys. Sewing. Beads.
11. Fastening coats. Shoes. Using spoons. Pencils.
12. Praise. Given opportunities. Range of toys. Objects of interest.

Further information
Physical Development by Jean Evans, Goals for the Foundation Stage series (Scholastic, 2003)
Physical Development by Pauline Kenyon, Around the Year series (Scholastic, 2001)

C5 Promote children's social and emotional development

This Unit focuses on the role of the worker in relation to the social and emotional development of children.

This chapter will help you to:

C5.1 Enable children to adjust to the setting
C5.2 Enable children to relate to others
C5.3 Develop children's self-reliance and self-esteem
C5.4 Enable children to recognise and deal with their feelings
C5.5 Enable children to develop a positive self-image and identity
C5.6 Prepare children to move on to new settings.

Element C5.1 Enable children to adjust to the setting

➤ Your assessor can observe and question you. · ◄ **C5.1**: range 1a, b, c, 2a

Plan a settling-in routine
Number of children: individual children or whole group.

Resources
Extra practitioners; materials according to the chosen activity.

Preparation
Invite the new children and their parents to the setting, prior to starting. Draw up a settling-in policy and plan for the child, on a one-to-one basis, and the whole group. This may include home visits. Invite new parents to an 'open' session. Prepare the room prior to the children arriving.

What to do
➤ Greet the parents and children as they arrive, using their preferred names.
➤ Show the children the coat hooks and toilets.
➤ If there are several children, begin the session by sitting on the carpet together. Alternatively, encourage them to participate in the regular routine.
➤ Introduce the members of staff.
➤ Call out the children's names and give them a name badge.
➤ Introduce the children to the activities in small groups.
➤ Explain the rules and encourage parents to assist their children. Allow a child to stand and observe if they are not ready to join in.

> ✔ **Tip**
>
> ➤ Advise parents and carers to teach their child to dress and undress, and do up buttons and zips in preparation for starting school.
>
> **C5.1**: 8
>
> ➤ Recommend that parents read books to their children about starting at the appropriate setting, to familiarise them with the routines and expectations.
>
> **C5.1**: 9

➤ Answer any parent's questions – refer to another practitioner if necessary.

➤ Choose a fun session to help the children feel comfortable.

➤ Let the children take home any craftwork they made during the session.

Support and extension

➤ *Cross-reference to* · · · ·
P2

Be on hand to reassure less confident children. Introduce the children to each ◀ other and, if appropriate, pair confident children with any less confident.

Evaluation

Do the setting's policies and procedures need revising? Did the activities engage the children? Would other activities have been better? Were you able to answer any questions? Do you need to know more about the policies?

Supporting activities

Assess the setting from the perspective of non-English speaking parents and children. As a group exercise with your colleagues, try to explain how you spent the last evening without using words.

Case study

➤ **C5.1**: 4 · · · · · · · ·

Lucy's mother is anxious about her starting full-time, in case she finds it a ◀ long day. She expects Lucy to come home tired and grumpy. What is the setting's policy for dealing with this? How will you reassure Lucy's mother? Write down the case study with your responses for your portfolio.

Follow on

➤ **C5.1**: 10 · · · · · · ·

Plan a routine that allows adequate time for quiet activities and rest. ◀ Discuss children's sleeping patterns with parents and carers and if they prefer quiet activities at particular times. Ensure there is a quiet corner where children can go, particularly during the settling-in period.

Questions

(See answer pointers at end of chapter.)

➤ **C5.1**: 5 · · · · · · · · ·
➤ **C5.1**: 7, 8 · · · · · · · ·
➤ **C5.1**: 9 · · · · · · · · ·

1. *How can you and your colleagues make children feel welcome?* ◀
2. *What activities can you suggest that do not depend on spoken language.* ◀
3. *Describe ways to share relevant information with parents about their child's* ◀ *adjustment, behaviour and enjoyment during the first days in a new setting.*

Record the questions and your answers and share these with your assessor.

Did you know?

Research shows that children cope well being looked after by several adult carers over a period of time, provided that in times of distress or tiredness they are with those with whom they have a secure attachment.

C5.1: 3, 5, 7

Extra idea

➤ **C5.1**: 6, 8 · · · · · · ·

Help shy or hesitant children settle into new surroundings by arranging the ◀ room to provide 'safe areas', separate from the main room.

Element C5.2 Enable children to relate to others

➤ Your assessor can observe and question you. · · · · · · · · · · · · · · · · · · · *C5.2*: *range 1d* ◄

Garden centre
Number of children: four.

Resources
Tables; toy cash register; money; plant pots; small garden tools; artificial flowers; flower wrapping paper; envelopes; flower and vegetable pictures; scissors; glue; garden catalogues; compost; quick growing cress or grass seeds; watering can; water; paper; felt-tipped pens.

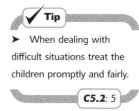

✔ **Tip**

➤ When dealing with difficult situations treat the children promptly and fairly.

C5.2: 5

Preparation
Plan the activity using the 'Activity plan' photocopiable sheet (page 131). Set the role-play area as a garden centre. Prepare shop signs, such as 'Pay here'.

What to do
➤ Allow the children to explore the area and develop spontaneous play.
➤ Introduce new words such as 'seed', 'compost' and 'germination'.
➤ Encourage the children to make things to 'sell' in the garden centre.
➤ Let the children make seed packets by gluing flower pictures on to envelopes.
➤ Wrap artificial flowers in paper for the fresh flower area.
➤ Invite the children to take on the roles of shoppers and servers.
➤ Ask one child to put compost in a pot, a second to sprinkle seeds on the compost and a third to water the seeds and serve the fourth, the customer.

Support and extension
Separate the seed and cutting sessions from the role-play corner with younger children. Invite older children to create their own price tickets, signs and plant care instructions, such as 'Water every day'.

Evaluation
➤ Did all the children participate, co-operate, relate well to one another and · · · *Cross-reference to* ◄
stay in role? Did the activity encourage any anti-social behaviour? Should you **C11**
have started with fewer props, gradually increasing them as the children
looked for new challenges? Were their language skills developed?

Supporting activity
➤ Invite the children to curl into little seeds, gradually unfurling until they are · · *Cross-reference to* **C3** ◄
fully-grown plants, waving their arms like leaves in the air.

➤ **C5.2**: 5 · · · · · · · · · ·

Case study

Mrs Morris makes a complaint after her daughter, Fallon, returns from the setting one day. Mrs Morris claims that Jack, another child from the group, said that 'black girls aren't allowed to play with special things'. Mrs Morris is very angry. How will you respond to Mrs Morris, Fallon, Jack and Jack's parents? How will you ensure this situation does not occur again? Write down the case study with your responses for your portfolio.

Follow on

➤ **C5.2**: range 2a · · · · ·

Look at the roles of the adults in the setting and how they can encourage children to relate to one another and respect each other. Is there a policy or procedure to address racism? Racist language, as with all language, is learned through contact and interaction with peers and significant adults.

Questions

(See answer pointers at end of chapter.)

➤ **C5.2**: 1 · · · · · · · · · **4.** *Identify a range of activities that encourage children to play co-operatively.* ◄

➤ **C5.2**: 4, 5 · · · · · · · · **5.** *Describe what anti-social behaviour is and how you can deal with it.* ◄

➤ **C5.2**: 8 · · · · · · · · · **6.** *Give examples of moral concepts you expect young children to be aware of.* ◄

Record the questions and your answers and share these with your assessor.

Did you know?

Psychologists offer 'modelling theory' as an explanation for children's behaviour. Children who spend considerable time with particular adults model their own behaviour, both positive and negative, on them. The way you behave will have an impact on the children in your care.

C5.2: 7

Extra idea

Copy the photocopiable 'Spider chart' on page 132. Write 'Relate to others' in the centre and activities to help communication in the surrounding boxes.

Element C5.3 Develop children's self-reliance and self-esteem

➤ **C5.3**: range 1a, b, c · · Your assessor can observe and question you.   ◄

Name this house

Number of children: four.

Resources

'Housey housey' photocopiable sheet on page 135; seven sheets of A4 card.

Preparation

Plan the activity using the 'Activity plan' photocopiable sheet on page 131. Make 24 small cards by cutting up three of the A4 sheets of card into eight, approximately 7.5cm by 10.5cm. Make six copies of the 'Housey housey' photocopiable sheet. Cut out each home and glue six assorted homes in two rows of three on the four remaining sheets of A4 card to form 'Housey housey' game cards. Mount individual homes on the small cards.

What to do
➤ Discuss the different types of homes with the children.
➤ Ask the children to identify the type of home they live in.
➤ Point out the positive aspects of each home, such as having your neighbours close by and not having to go upstairs to bed.
➤ Stack the small cards face down and give each child a game card.
➤ Explain to the children that they are going to play a matching game.
➤ Invite the first child to pick a card and try to match the home to their game card. If it doesn't match, ask them to pass the card to the next player.
➤ The first child to cover all their six homes is the winner.

Support and extension
Help the younger children to match the homes to their game card without undermining their self-confidence. With older children, discuss how other people live. Let the children make their own decisions.

Evaluation
Did you handle the discussions in a sensitive way? Were the children able to relate to the homes? Did they take turns? Were they kind to one another? Did they take an interest in each other? Did you feel confident in leading the discussion? Did you listen to the children and encourage them to communicate?

Supporting activity
Show the children pictures and discuss housing around the world.

> ✔ **Tip**
> ➤ Allow children to express themselves and make their own decisions. Too much guidance hampers development.
> **C5.3**: 3

➤ ### Case study
Practitioners in the setting are concerned about Lizzie's progress as she has difficulties with her self-help skills. She sits and waits for an adult to dress her and does not feed herself. What may be the cause of this behaviour? How can you help Lizzie overcome these difficulties? Write down the case study with your responses for your portfolio.

C5.3: 4, 5, 7, 9 ◄

➤ ### Follow on
For a one-week period, make a record of every time a child has been given a choice or has made their own decision. As a reflective account write up your observations and evaluation. Having raised your awareness consider if you can increase the occasions for decision making, particularly with children experiencing difficulty with self-reliance and self-esteem.

C5.3: 3, 6, 8 ◄

Questions
(See answer pointers at end of chapter.)
➤ **7.** *How can you ensure children's needs are listened to and positively dealt with?* **C5.3**: 1 ◄
➤ **8.** *Identify self-help skills in the daily routine that children can expect to achieve.* **C5.3**: 4 ◄

➤ **C5.3**: 8 · · · · · · · · **9.** *What common assumptions reinforce stereotypes and damage self-esteem?* ◄

Record the questions and your answers and share these with your assessor.

Did you know?
Research has shown that there are positive benefits for bilingual children in addition to language learning. There is evidence to suggest an increased problem-solving ability, a more positive identity and an increased self-esteem.

Extra ideas
➤ **C5.3**: 4 · · · · · · · · Reinforce self-esteem through role-play. ◄
➤ **C5.3**: 3 · · · · · · · · Make children responsible for selecting a book or looking after pets. ◄

Element C5.4 Enable children to recognise and deal with their feelings

➤ **C5.4**: *range 1b,* · · · · Your assessor can observe and question you. ◄
2a, b

Happy and sad faces
Number of children: four.

Resources
Paper plates or circles of card; skin tone crayons; collage materials to make facial features; wool or crêpe-paper strips; rulers; glue; scissors; sticky tape.

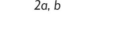

➤ Tell stories that include different emotions. Relate incidents from your early life that had an effect on you. Encourage children to share their times of happiness and sadness.

C5.4: 4

Preparation
Plan the activity using the 'Activity plan' photocopiable sheet on page 131. Sit the group around a table.

What to do
➤ Discuss feelings and ask the children how they feel at certain times, for example when they receive a present or when a toy breaks.
➤ Encourage the children to each select two paper plates or circles of card and colour them in to make two faces – one happy and one sad.
➤ Let the children glue collage materials to the circles as features .
➤ Help the children tape a ruler to the back of the circle to hold the puppet.

Support and extension
Assist younger children to attach the features and ruler. Encourage older children to include more facial details, such as eyebrows and hair accessories.

Evaluation
Did the children discuss their feelings? Will you make any changes if you repeat this session? Should this activity be part of a theme about 'Ourselves'? Explain your answers. Discuss the outcome with your assessor.

Supporting activities

➤ Use the face puppets to tell a story during circle time. Use additional props · · **C5.4**: *1, 3, 6* ◄
and a simple puppet theatre to act out scenarios addressing emotional issues.

Case study

➤ Four-year-old Zoë snatches toys from other children and screams if they   **C5. 4**: *5* ◄
try to retrieve them. She has difficulty expressing herself in words; her
parents guess what she means by her body language, but see no urgency
in dealing with the situation. How do you think this should be
approached? Write down the case study with your responses for your
portfolio.

Follow on

➤ Consider the reasons why children are unable to express their feelings in   **C5. 4**: *5* ◄
words. Include disabilities, emotional issues, inconsistent handling, fear,
English as a second language, Autistic Spectrum Disorder and being too
young. Find out about these aspects and the ways you can help
overcome them.

Questions

(See answer pointers at end of chapter.)

➤ **10.** *What methods and activities can you suggest to explore feelings?* · · · · · · **C5.4**: *3* ◄
➤ **11.** *How can you help a frustrated child who is unable to communicate easily?* **C5.4**: *4* ◄
➤ **12.** *What actions can you take if you are concerned about particular feelings*   **C5.4**: *7* ◄
expressed by individual children?

Record the questions and your answers and share these with your assessor.

Did you know?

It is sometimes assumed that children in the early years are too young
to experience stress. While they may not understand the reasons, they
are aware of stressful situations and react accordingly. Showing anxiety
teaches anxiety. Offer a stress-free environment where a child feels
safe and secure. A calm, consistent approach, where feelings can be
expressed, will ease stress.

C5.4: *2*

Extra idea

Using the photocopiable 'Spider chart' on page 132, write 'Feelings' in the
centre. In each box write an example of an emotion.

Element C5.5 Enable children to develop a positive self-image and identity

➤ Your assessor can observe and question you. · **C5.5**: *range 1a, b, c, d,* ◄
e, f

Mirror, mirror in the box

Number of children: whole group.

✔ Tip

➤ Give positive feedback to children for whom English is an additional language when they attempt to speak. Use non-verbal communication, and many interjections such as 'good girl', 'well done' and 'great'.

C5.5: 1

Resources
Small gift box with lid; mirror; double-sided sticky tape.

Preparation
Plan the activity using the 'Activity plan' photocopiable sheet on page 131. Fix the mirror on the inside base of the gift box with sticky tape.

What to do
➤ Invite the children to sit in a circle on the carpet.
➤ Tell the children a story about a special person, or read *All Kinds of People* by Emma Damon (Tango Books, 1997).
➤ Explain that you are going to show the children a special gift in the box, but ask them to keep it a secret until the end.
➤ Invite each child to come forward in turn, open the box and look inside.
➤ When everyone has had a turn ask the children what was in the box. Did everyone see the same thing. If not, ask them to explain what was different?
➤ Reassure the children that they are special.

Support and extension
Keep groups small with younger children and encourage with smiles and reassurance. Build up the tension for older children to make it more exciting. Discuss the individual children, their gender, physical features and clothes.

Evaluation
Did you use opportunities to discuss similarities and differences? What other activities may develop the concept of 'self'? Did the discussion reveal anything you were not aware of? Will you follow this up?

Supporting activities
➤ **C5.5**: 2 · · · · · · · · Introduce a series of activities about 'ourselves'. Read stories about children ◄ in unfamiliar circumstances and environments.

Case study
➤ **C5.5**. 7, range 1b · · When Milly is asked what she thinks she says she does not know. She ◄ tries to conform to the setting rules, is distressed if she breaks the rules inadvertently and spends most of the session in solitary play. Her parents comment if Milly has marked her clothing or lost her hairslide. How can you resolve this situation? Write down the case study with your responses for your portfolio.

Follow on
➤ **C5.5**: 9 · · · · · · · · Find out what the setting policy is on referrals. Who can you seek advice ◄ from and their role is?

Questions
(See answer pointers at end of chapter.)
➤ **C5.5**: 3, 5 · · · · · · · **13.** *Give examples of non-stereotypical play and positive images to be found in* ◄ *a setting, and how you can promote these.*

➤ **14.** *Who can you invite to the setting to promote positive role models and why?* · · · · **C5.5**: 4 ◀
➤ **15.** *What are the signs of low self-image and disturbed development of self-identity?* · · **C5.5**: 7 ◀

Record the questions and your answers and share these with your assessor.

Did you know?
Article 30 of the United Nations Convention on the Rights of the Child states, '...a child belonging to such a minority or who is indigenous shall not be denied the right, in community with other members of his or her group, to enjoy his or her own culture, to profess and practice his or her own religion, or to use his or her own language'.

C5.5: 6

Extra idea
Invite the children to keep 'life story' books. Begin with a photo of the child, add paintings of themselves and their home and interests. Request family photos from home. Let older children write about themselves.

Element C5.6 Prepare children to move on to new settings

➤ Your assessor can observe and question you. · · · · · · · · · · · · · · · · · **C5.6**: range 1a, b, d, ◀
2a, b

Sharing cultures
Children may move on to settings where they will meet unfamiliar children with different customs. Try to raise their awareness of different cultures.
Number of children: four.

Resources
Non-fiction and story-books about children from different cultures; posters and photos of diverse families; ethnically-diverse dressing-up clothes and dolls; cooking utensils and play food from a variety of cultures; 'Religious and cultural designs' photocopiable sheet on page 136; scissors; card; glue.

Preparation
Plan the activity using the 'Activity plan' photocopiable sheet on page 131. On different occasions you can vary the resources you use. Enlarge the 'Religious and cultural designs' photocopiable sheet for each child.

What to do
➤ Over a period of time introduce the children to the idea of meeting other children, who may look, dress and eat differently to them.
➤ Using books, posters and photos, discuss children from diverse cultures.
➤ Role-play with cooking utensils, play food and dressing-up clothes.
➤ Discuss the designs on the photocopiable sheet. Invite the children to colour them in, cut them out and glue them on card.
➤ Encourage the children to ask questions and provide further information.
➤ If appropriate, arrange to go to the new setting to allay any fears.

Tip

➤ Any information given out about children must be within the setting's strict guidelines of confidentiality.

C5.6: 7

Support and extension

Discuss the physical environment that the children will be going to and answer any questions they have. Invite a member of staff from the new setting to visit. Explain what you have been doing with your group so that informed answers can be given to the children's questions.

Evaluation

Do you feel the children gained any insight into the differences and similarities between the cultural groups? Could you answer the children's questions? Is there anything else you can do? Discuss with your assessor.

Supporting activities

Identify how many children will be moving to the new setting at the same time. Ask all the children to draw a picture of themselves and attach to a display board alongside pictures of other children who will be in the same setting.

➤ **C5.6**: 1 · · · · · · · ·

Case study

Charlie is fearful to move from his childminder to Reception. His parents are not worried as their friends' children have been fine, so they are not taking time off work. As the childminder, you want the best for Charlie. What will you do? Write down the case study with your responses for your portfolio.

Follow on

How can you alleviate children's fears, whether they are about spiders, ghosts or school? Be one step ahead of the children and prepared to answer questions or provide appropriate activities. Discuss their fears, offer reassurance and comfort. Never belittle a child for being afraid.

Questions

(See answer pointers at end of chapter.)

➤ **C5.6**: 1 · · · · · · · · ·   **16.** *Who can help prepare a child and arrange for a move to a new setting?*

➤ **C5.6**: 5 · · · · · · · · ·   **17.** *What activities can you plan to prepare a child to move to a new setting?*

➤ **C5.6**: 6 · · · · · · · · ·   **18.** *What opportunities may arise to familiarise a child with a new setting?*

Record the questions and your answers and share these with your assessor.

Did you know?

People say that 'all children are the same'. In fact all children are different. Try not to make assumptions and remember to treat every one as an individual. It is also assumed that we have multicultural play, multicultural food and multicultural children. The word 'multicultural' is a collective noun referring to objects, so we have multicultural play and food from different cultures, but a child only has its own cultural experiences.

Extra idea
➤ Cut out the front of a cardboard box to look like a television with knobs on · · **C5.6**: 3, 4   ◄
the front. Ask two children to sit with their head and shoulders inside and let
them talk about their concerns about a new setting. Listen and respond.

Practical ways of collecting evidence
Emotional and social development occurs throughout all the activities, every
day. Ensure all the assessor's direct observations have been recorded as
evidence for this Unit. Children need praise and encouragement to boost
their self-esteem. This in turn gives them confidence to do other things.

Check your progress
To complete this Unit you need to be directly observed by your assessor
for at least one aspect of each range statement in each of the six
Elements. Your assessor may not see all the performance criteria so you
may have to collect evidence by other means. Be ready to discuss your
setting's policies on special needs, settling in, confidentiality, parental
involvement and equal opportunities.

Answer pointers
Ensure your answers are fully made for your assessor.
1. Preparation. Names. Picture identification on pegs. Smile. Calm.
2. Construction toys. Painting. Sand. Water. Snakes and ladders.
3. Discuss. Home-school book. Send home paintings. Telephone. Video links.
4. Role-play. Games. Helping each other. Partners in PE. Tidying up.
5. Physical harm. Hurt feelings. Insults. Racism. Damage to items. Stealing.
Talk. Discuss. Situational books. Boost self-esteem. Puppets.
6. Right and wrong. Respect. Accept others' needs. Look after possessions.
7. Being aware. Giving time. Giving awards (stickers). Public praise.
8. Dressing. Feeding. Toileting. Setting table. Hand washing. Selecting toys.
9. 'Boys don't cry'. 'Disability means you can't do'. 'Boys don't cook'.
10. Dolls. Home corner. Drama. Puppets. Books. Stories.
11. Language. Interpretation. Speech therapy. Time. Listening. Singing.
12. Policies. Guidance. Listen. Report. Observe.
13. Posters. Photographs. Dressing-up. Dolls. Boys and girls. Toys.
14. Female vicar. Signer. Black policeman. Female fire fighter.
15. Dislike of self. Scrubbing dark skin. Rejecting other disabled people.
Denying racial origins. Refusing to speak in heritage language.
16. Parents. Practitioners. Colleagues.
17. Drawings. Painting. Role-play. Story telling. Puppets.
18. Talking. Visits. Passing by. Photographs.

Further information
Helping Children Build Self-esteem by Deborah Plummer (Jessica Kingsley
Publishers, 2002)

C7 Provide a framework for the management of behaviour

This Unit provides a framework for all aspects of children's behaviour. It covers positive behaviour, how to manage unwanted behaviour, goals and boundary setting. It also looks at social, physical and verbal behaviour, directly challenging carers, disruptive behaviour, self-damaging and aggressive acts.

This chapter will enable you to:

C7.1 Negotiate and set goals and boundaries for behaviour
C7.2 Promote positive aspects of behaviour
C7.3 Respond to unwanted behaviour.

Element C7.1 Negotiate and set goals and boundaries for behaviour

➤ **C7.1**: *range 1a, c* · · · · Your assessor can observe and question you. ◄

Tip

➤ A goal is behaviour you want a child to aim for. A boundary is the limit of acceptable behaviour within the setting.

C7.1: 1, 2, 3, 4, 5

Play dough in partnership
Number of children: four.

Resources
'Play dough recipes' photocopiable sheet on page 137; appropriate ingredients; mixing bowl; jug; water; cup; tablespoon; wooden spoon; aprons; table cover.

Preparation
Plan the activity using the 'Activity plan' photocopiable sheet on page 131. Set up the area and invite the children to stand or sit around the work surface.

What to do
➤ Find out if anyone knows how to make play dough.
➤ Invite each child to measure out the different ingredients.
➤ Follow the recipe and let the children take turns mixing the ingredients.
➤ Flour the work surface and give the children some dough to play with.

Support and extension
Help younger children measure and mix the ingredients. Let older children choose the colour.

Evaluation
Did the children share the tasks and wait for their turn? Were they kind to each other and did they follow the rules? Did the children actively take part?

early years
training &
management

Supporting activity

➤ Use play dough in the home corner as play food with rolling-pins, blunt · · · · knives, patty tins, a chakla (board) for making chapattis and velma (roller).

Cross-reference to **C3**, ◄
C10

Case study

➤ Three-year-old Lauren is possessive over toys, claiming one doll and screaming if anyone comes near it. You have not intervened as you hoped she would settle. She has not. How will you deal with this situation? Write down the case study with your responses for your portfolio.

C7.1: 1, 2, 4, 5 ◄

Follow on

In order to function cohesively, boundaries must be set in the interests of the group as a whole. List the boundaries within your setting, or those that you feel would be appropriate. Discuss these with your assessor.

Questions
(See answer pointers at end of chapter.)

➤ **1.** *Suggest forms of emotional behaviour in a group of five- to eight-year-olds.*   *C7.1*: 1 ◄
➤ **2.** *Why is it important to agree on the setting's goals and boundaries?* · · · · · ·   *C7.1*: 2 ◄
➤ **3.** *In what ways can cultural influences affect the behaviour of a child?* · · · · · ·   *C7.1*: 3 ◄

Record the questions and your full answers and share these with your assessor.

Did you know?

You can buy achievement stickers to acknowledge good behaviour. These are a useful means of acknowledging the meeting of goals.

C7.1: 5

Extra idea

➤ Ask the children to write up the rules of the setting and display them at child height on a notice board. Have more 'Do' rules than 'Don't' rules.

C7.1: 4 ◄

Element C7.2 Promote positive aspects of behaviour

➤ Your assessor can observe and question you. · · · · · · · · · · · · · · · · · · ·   *C7.2*: range 1a ◄

Banana buddies
Number of children: four.

Resources
Aprons; bananas; lolly sticks; blunt knife; plates or cutting boards; cling film; freezer bag and tie; use of a freezer.

Preparation
Plan the activity using the 'Activity plan' photocopiable sheet on page 131. Check for any food allergies or dietary requirements.

✔ Tip

➤ Use good behaviour diaries or reward charts for all children (see photocopiable 'Reward chart' on page 138). Acknowledge positive actions with a star, sticker, ink stamper or by colouring in.

C7.2: 6

What to do

➤ Ask the children to wash their hands thoroughly and put on their aprons.
➤ Help the children peel the bananas and cut a 6cm length.
➤ Let the children push lolly sticks into the bananas.
➤ Invite the children to wrap the banana buddies in cling film and place them all carefully in a freezer bag. Leave in the freezer for one hour.
➤ Share the banana buddies with the rest of the group at snack time.

Support and extension

➤ *Cross-reference to* · ·
C2

Let younger children make their own banana buddies, but prepare more for ◄ the group. Invite older children to prepare further snacks on future days.

Evaluation

Did the children feel special as they were sharing with everyone? Would you change the activity if you did it again? What other snacks can you suggest?

Supporting activity

Let the children make gifts for parents, look after new children, tidy up when asked, collect the register and give out milk.

➤ **C7.2**: *1, 3, 5* · · · · · ·

Case study

You are planning a session to emphasise playing co-operatively. Penny ◄ often plays on her own and you want to attract her into the group. What activities can you provide? How can you promote positive behaviour? Write down the case study with your responses for your portfolio.

➤ **C7.2**: *1* · · · · · · · ·

Follow on

Make a file of games to encourage co-operative play. Start with 'Ring-a-ring ◄ o' roses' and build up to more elaborate ring games. Add notes about variations that you have devised, or advice, such as 'best suited to outdoors'.

Questions

(See answer pointers at end of chapter.)

➤ **C7.2**: *3* · · · · · · · ·
4. *What constitutes positive behaviour? Identify the type of behaviour you* ◄ *expect and how you can explain this to the children.*

➤ **C7.2**: *5* · · · · · · · ·
5. *In what ways can you share positive aspects of behaviour with parents and* ◄ *colleagues to enhance the children's self-esteem?*

➤ **C7.2**: *6* · · · · · · · ·
6. *What rewards can you suggest for recognising positive behaviour?* ◄

Record the questions and your full answers and share these with your assessor.

Did you know?

It takes around 43 muscles to frown, but only 17 to smile. This makes smiling so much easier.

Extra idea

➤ **C7.2**: *5, 6* · · · · · · ·
List aspects of positive behaviour and an incident from your own experience. ◄ For example, 'Be sensitive – to a child whose parents were divorcing'.

Element C7.3 Respond to unwanted behaviour

➤ Your assessor can observe and question you. · **C7.3**: range 1a, b, c, ◄
d, e

Situational story-telling

Number of children: one-to-one with a child exhibiting unwanted behaviour.

Resources
Relevant fiction book or story-book addressing the specific issue being experienced.

Preparation
Plan the activity using the 'Activity plan' photocopiable sheet on page 131. Find out about the background of the particular child, to personalise the story.

What to do
➤ Ensure the child is sitting comfortably with the minimum of distractions.
➤ Use real-life situations that can be responded to, such as going shopping.
➤ Adjust the story slightly to fit the particular circumstances.
➤ Introduce an example of the behaviour, such as shouting or bullying.
➤ Ask the child to suggest how to deal with the situation.
➤ End on a positive note with a resolution to the unwanted behaviour.

Support and extension
Tell the story to younger children several times over. Raise the issue of the real unwanted behaviour with older children.

Evaluation
Did the story gain the child's attention? Was it pitched at the right level? Did you get a positive response from the child? Do you need to practise your story-telling techniques? Did this help reduce the unwanted behaviour?

Supporting activity
Tell situational stories to the whole group. Encourage the children to listen before commenting. Ask them to suggest possible resolutions to the issues.

✔ Tip

➤ Adults need to be good role models. If the adults shout so will the children. Be aware of your own actions.

C7.3: 5

Case study
➤ William's father brings him to nursery, saying, 'If he doesn't behave himself today, give him a smack. I've had enough. I've told him you will smack him if he doesn't behave'. Suggest reasons for William's behaviour? Will you carry out his father's wishes? How will you deal with the situation? Write down the case study with your responses for your portfolio.

C7.3: 1, 4, 5, 7, 9 ◄

Follow on
Consider the different ways to manage children's behaviour, such as facial expressions, supervision, eye contact, patience, praise and as a role model.

Questions
(See answer pointers at end of chapter.)

➤ **C7.3**: 2, 5, 6 · · · · · **7.** *A new three-year-old loves getting out all the toys, but is unwilling to put* ◀
them back again. How can you encourage this child to put things away?

➤ **C7.3**: 3 · · · · · · · · **8.** *Give examples of sanctions directed at the unwanted behaviour not the child.* ◀

➤ **C7.3**: 5 · · · · · · · · **9.** *What are the contributing factors that may provoke unwanted behaviour?* ◀

Record the questions and your full answers and share these with your assessor.

Did you know?
Signs of bullying include a reluctance to go to the setting, frequent
complaints of illness when it is time to leave, unexplained injuries,
delayed language development, behaviour regression and bouts of
tearfulness.

C7.3: 4

Extra idea
Copy the 'All in good time' photocopiable sheet on page 139. Ask the
children to answer the questions with a smiley or sad face.

Practical ways of collecting evidence

➤ Cross-reference to · · Management of behaviour will be seen by your assessor during direct ◀
C16 observations. Ensure it is recorded and cross-referenced to this Unit. If a child
displays unusual or excessive behaviour, observe them over time, recording
your observations. Evaluate the results to establish the frequency and triggers.

Check your progress
To complete this Unit you will need to be directly observed by your
assessor for at least one aspect of each range statement in each of the
three Elements. Your assessor may not see all the performance criteria
so you may have to use other means, such as reflective accounts. Your
assessor may question you on your setting's policies.

Answer pointers
Ensure your answers are fully made for your assessor.
1. Teasing. Refuse to let play. Withdraw friendship. Deny use of equipment.
2. Consistency. Reinforcement. Parental wishes. Fairness.
3. Late nights. Physical punishment. Noisy. Different table manners.
4. Co-operation. Contributing. Helping. Sharing. Concentrating. Complying.
5. Praise parents and colleagues. Recognise positive behaviour. Positive
reinforcement. Good behaviour diary.
6. Star charts. Ink stampers. Wall displays with names. Tangible rewards.
7. Reason with. Make a game. Pair with older child. Make fun.
8. Remove from area. Withdraw privileges. Redirect to other activities.
9. Allergic reactions. New sibling. Bereavement. Death of pet. Separation.

Further information
Time to Listen to Children by Pat Milner and Birgit Carolin (Routledge, 1999)

C10 Promote children's sensory and intellectual development

This Unit focuses on memory, concentration, sensory awareness, mathematics, science, creativity and the imagination. Children with impairments are an integral part of this Unit.

This chapter will enable you to:
C10.1 Develop children's attention span and memory
C10.2 Develop children's awareness and understanding of sensory experiences
C10.3 Develop children's understanding of mathematics and science
C10.4 Develop children's imagination and creativity.

Element C10.1 Develop children's attention span and memory

➤ Your assessor can observe and question you. · **C10.1**: *range 1a* ◄

Kim's game
Number of children: six.

Resources
Tray; small objects from the setting; tea towel; cardboard box with a lid.

Preparation
Plan the activity using the 'Activity plan' photocopiable sheet on page 131. Out of sight of the children place the objects on the tray, evenly spaced apart, and cover with the tea towel.

What to do
➤ Invite the children to sit comfortably around the table.
➤ Explain that they are going to play a memory game.
➤ Place the tray in the centre of the table. Remove the cloth and ask the children to look carefully at the objects for one minute, then re-cover with the cloth.
➤ Encourage the children to close their eyes tightly, without peeping.
➤ Remove one object, put it in the box and cover the objects again.
➤ Let the children open their eyes and remove the cover again. Ask the children, in turn, if they know which item is missing.
➤ Repeat this until all the objects have been removed.

Support and extension

With younger children, use a few, easily identifiable everyday objects. For older children, use a greater number of unusual items.

Evaluation

Did you select the right number of items? Did you allow long enough for the children to see and recall the items? How can you vary the objects? Did the children lose interest? Share your thoughts with your assessor.

Supporting activity

Choose objects that are relevant to your current theme. For example, for the theme of light, choose a selection of different types of lights.

➤ **C10.1**: 1, 6, 7, 8 · ·

Case study

Four-year-old Ravi has a short concentration span. He does not settle at any activity for more than a few seconds. His only passion is football. He knows all the names of his favourite team, can tell you the score for the past few matches and wants to kick a ball around all day. How can you help develop Ravi's attention and concentration using the knowledge you have about him? Write down the case study with your responses for your portfolio.

➤ **C10.1**: 5, 6, 8, · ·
cross-reference to
C10.3

Follow on

During circle time find out the interests of the children. Ask them to give one interest each and discuss the reasons for their choice, using their own experience and memory recall. Ask the children to draw a single representation of their favourite activity on a small square of paper. Make a bar graph (see illustration) with the interests along the horizontal axis and the number of children on the vertical axis. Fix the drawings to the chart to see which interest is the overall favourite. Use the results for future planning.

Questions

(See answer pointers at end of chapter.)

➤ **1.** *Suggest activities that develop children's attention span and memory.* · · · · · **C10.1**: *1*   ◀
➤ **2.** *Why develop children's memory recall and prediction of events?* · · · · · · · · **C10.1**: *5*   ◀
➤ **3.** *How can we maintain and extend children's attention span and memory?* · · **C10.1**: *8*   ◀

Record the questions and your full answers and share these with your assessor.

Did you know?

Millions of nerve cells (neurons) are thought to be involved in the recall of memory. Adults have the same number of nerve cells as babies. No matter how long we live, we will never have more. By old age many will have died, which is why memory is often poor in the elderly.

Extra idea

➤ As a regular part of the routine, ask questions about what the children did · · **C10.1**: *6*   ◀
yesterday, what the weather was like and what Monday's story was about.

Element C10.2 Develop children's awareness and understanding of sensory experiences

➤ Your assessor can observe and question you. · **C10.2**: *range 1c, 2b,*   ◀
3a

Feely resource book

Number of children: six.

Resources

Ring binder; A4 sheets of card; hole-punch; glue; sticky tape; scissors (adult use); assorted textured materials, such as velvet, wool, muslin, nylon, aluminium foil, sandpaper, textured wallpaper, nylon fur, string and tinsel.

Preparation

Plan the activity using the 'Activity plan' photocopiable sheet on page 131. Punch holes in the card to fit in the file. Cut the materials to10cms x 20cms.

What to do

➤ Offer the children the sheets of card and a choice of textured materials.
➤ Invite the children to feel the materials and discuss the different textures as a group. Introduce appropriate words, such as soft, smooth and crinkly.
➤ Let the children take a sheet of card each and glue a piece of material to it. They can either glue it flat or just at the top, so it can be lifted and felt.
➤ Ask the children to choose a contrasting texture for a second card.
➤ Place all the cards in the file in the quiet area. Show the children where they are and explain that they can go there to look at and feel the textures.

Support and extension

Help younger children stick the materials on securely. Let older children cut the materials. Invite literate children to write descriptive words on the card.

✔ Tip

➤ Before tasting, smelling and, depending on the material used, touching unfamiliar objects, you must get permission from the parents and carers to ensure children are not allergic to the substances.

➤ On occasions choose more unusual fruit and vegetables for the children to try. Some children may find them familiar, others will never have had the opportunity to see, handle or taste them.

C10.2: *2*

Evaluation

➤ *Cross-reference to* · · Did the children enjoy the activity? Did it stimulate discussion and the use of ◄
C24   familiar and unfamiliar words? Can you think of additional textures to add to
                                 the 'texture file'? Did the session spark other ideas for textural activities?

Supporting activity

Make a textural bingo game with six squares of different materials mounted
on four A5 cards. Make sure the materials are in different places on each card
and ensure there are the same number of corresponding squares in a bag.
The first child to collect all six pieces is the winner.

➤ **C10.2**: *1, 6, range* · ·
1a, b, c, d, e, 2a,
3b, cross-reference
to **M7**

Case study

You are planning a walk outside to develop sensory experiences. Sophie ◄
is four and has a visual impairment, but is interested in birds. What will you
consider when planning to ensure maximum sensory experiences for the
children? Write down the case study with your responses for your portfolio.

➤ **C10.2**: *1* · · · · · · ·

Follow on

Use the environment around your setting as an opportunity to develop ◄
sensory awareness. Gardening, insects, plants and trees, weather, sounds
and pets, all help children to have good sensory experiences.

Questions

(See answer pointers at end of chapter.)

➤ **C10.2**: *2* · · · · · · · **4.** *Suggest unplanned opportunities to promote awareness of the senses.* ◄
➤ **C10.2**: *4* · · · · · · · **5.** *What terms can you introduce to help children name, talk about and reflect* ◄
                            on their sensory experiences?
➤ **C10.2**: *7* · · · · · · · **6.** *Can you think of two activities for each of the senses that you can plan for* ◄
                            babies, three-year-olds and seven-year-olds?

Record the questions and your full answers and share these with your assessor.

Did you know?

Children with cochlear implants may have difficulty using certain
equipment as the static electricity can affect the settings of the device.
To reduce friction, put fabric softener on a cloth and wipe particular
areas, such as slides and soft play equiment, every few days.

C10.2: 6

Extra ideas

➤ **C10.2**: *1* · · · · · · · Using the photocopiable 'Spider chart' on page 132, write 'Our senses' in the ◄
centre. Use the eight boxes to plan sessions to develop awareness and
understanding of sensory experiences covering each of the six Areas of
Learning, plus multicultural and displays.

➤ **C10.2**: *3* · · · · · · · Dissolve coloured jelly cubes, with a little extra water. Place clean plastic farm ◄
animals into the liquid jelly and place in bowls in the fridge until set. Allow
the children to experience this unusual tactile media.

Element C10.3 Develop children's understanding of mathematics and science

➤ Your assessor can observe and question you. · · · · · · · · · · · · · · · · · · · **C10.3**: range: 1b, 2a ◄

Cookie cookery
Number of children: six.

Resources
100g self-raising flour plus extra for sprinkling; 100g soft brown sugar; 38g soft margarine; 1tsp ground ginger; one egg; large bowl; small bowl; forks; blunt knives; large spoons; baking sheet; rice paper; food-colouring pen; aprons; weighing scales; anti-bacterial spray; use of oven.

Preparation
Plan the activity using the 'Activity plan' photocopiable sheet on page 131. Ask permission from parents and carers for the children to taste foods and check for any food allergies or dietary requirements. Thoroughly clean the work surface with anti-bacterial spray. Ensure the resources are ready, although the ingredients do not have to be weighed out at this stage. Set the oven to 180°C/350°F/Gas Mark 4.

What to do
➤ Ask the children to put on their aprons and thoroughly wash their hands.
➤ Invite the children to work in pairs. Suggest that one pair weighs the flour, one weighs the sugar and one weighs the margarine. Ask the pairs to put their ingredients into one bowl and then add the ginger.
➤ Encourage the children to take turns to mix the ingredients with a fork until the mixture becomes crumbly.
➤ Break the egg into a small bowl and ask the children to take turns mixing it with a fork.
➤ Add enough beaten egg to bind the mixture together.
➤ Sprinkle some flour on to the table in front of each child and divide the mixture into six equal parts, giving one to each child.
➤ Ask the children to knead the dough and roll it into a sausage shape.
➤ If appropriate, let the children cut their rolls into four equal-sized pieces. Invite them to roll each piece into a ball and place them on a greased baking sheet. Leave plenty of room between the cookies to allow for spreading. To ensure they cook evenly, use a fork to create small fork holes in each cookie.
➤ Ask the children to each write their name or initial on a tiny piece of rice paper with the food-colouring pen. Use a small amount of egg or milk to stick these to their cookies.
➤ Place the cookies in the oven and bake for 15 minutes. Enjoy them together at break time.

Support and extension
Be on hand to help younger children and show them what you mean

Tip

➤ Use the resources you have to explore relational concepts, such as big children and little children, big steps and little steps, big books and little books.

C10.3: 1

➤ Sand and water are the most versatile early years resources for teaching the scientific concepts of wet and dry, floating and sinking, hot and cold, and quantity.

C10.3: 4

throughout the session. Use language appropriate to their level of development. Talk to older children in greater detail about cleanliness, weight and balance, measurement, changes, division and temperature. See the 'Recipes' photocopiable sheet on page 140 for further ideas.

Evaluation

> *Cross-reference to* **C10.2, C2, C25**

Was this an appropriate activity for the age group? Did everything go smoothly or were there things you would do differently next time? Was safety observed at all times?

Supporting activity

Use different recipes to develop skills in science, mathematics and language development, as well as encouraging self-confidence, self-esteem and social skills. Appropriate cookery ideas include vegetable soup, jacket potatoes, bread, fruit salad, chocolate crispy cakes, peppermint creams and sandwiches.

> **C10.3**: *4, 5, 6*

Case study

Joshua is a very inquisitive child; his favourite word is 'why?'. One day he asks you where ice comes from. He is not content with a simple answer. You are not sure he fully understands the abstract concept so you decide to prepare an activity, later in the day, to demonstrate what happens to ice under different conditions. Share your ideas with your assessor. Write down the case study with your responses for your portfolio.

> **C10.3**: *6*

Follow on

Teaching science to young children is a matter of explaining, verbally and practically, the properties of everyday materials. Over a period of time, take note of all the questions of a scientific nature children have asked you or your colleagues. Do you know the answers to questions such as, 'How are bubbles made?' or, 'Why do leaves fall off trees?'. You may need to do some research to find the answers. Keep the information simple.

Questions

(See answer pointers at end of chapter.)

> **C10.3**: *1, 5*

7. *What are the relational concepts young children need to know and how can you get this information across in a way they can understand?*

> **C10.3**: *2*

8. *How can you be prepared for unplanned opportunities to extend children's understanding of relevant concepts? Give examples.*

> **C10.3**: *3, cross-reference to* **C17**

9. *In what ways can you adapt mathematics and science activities for a visually impaired child?*

Record the questions and your full answers and share these with your assessor.

Did you know?

Children need to be able to recognise patterns to understand mathematics. Look for patterns in your setting and the surrounding environment, such as bricks, paving slabs, windows, carpets, clothes, sand patterns and rows of toys.

C10.3: *2*

Extra ideas

➤ Set up a 'transparent' table display using articles requested from home. These could include coloured and clear glass bottles, reading and sun glasses, a magnifying glass, drinking glasses, a goldfish bowl, cling film, a light bulb, a clear paperweight and a bubble mix and wand.

C10.3: 5, 7 ◄

➤ Using the photocopiable 'Spider chart' on page 132, write 'Water' in the · · · centre and identify as many different ways of presenting water-related activities as you can. Create further boxes if you need to.

C10.3: 1, 2, 3, 4 ◄

Element C10.4 Develop children's imagination and creativity

➤ Your assessor can observe and question you. · *C10.4*: range 1b, 2c ◄

Shadow puppet show
Number of children: six.

Resources
Six sheets of thin A4 card; strong drinking straws; felt-tipped pens; sticky tape; scissors; cotton bed sheet; string; lamp; plug; electric socket.

Preparation
Plan the activity using the 'Activity plan' photocopiable sheet on page 131. Tie each corner of the sheet with string and suspend at child-height level with the sheet pulled taut; this is best across a corner of the room. Position the lamp behind at the same height as the sheet screen. Ensure the craft materials are ready on the table.

What to do
➤ Demonstrate how a shadow puppet works, using the outline suggested in the illustration. Show the children that it is the outside shape and any holes in the card that are significant.

➤ Give the children a sheet of card each and ask them to use felt-tipped pens to draw a figure or shape that nearly fills the card. Cut out the figures and any appropriate holes for the eyes, mouth and so on.

➤ Show the children how to stick straws to one side of their puppets, so they can hold and move them about.

➤ Switch on the lamp and ask the children to sit in front of the screen. Let all the children see their own puppets and the effects they make behind the screen.

➤ Encourage the children to make any adjustments to their puppets if they choose to.

➤ When the children are happy with their puppets, invite them to work in pairs and devise their own stories involving their puppets.

Support and extension
➤ Advise younger children on the appropriate shapes for shadow puppets. Keep it simple. Alternatively, supply a range of puppet templates for them to use.

C10.4: 10 ◄

> **Tip**

➤ Check that all the materials used are safe and suitable for the planned activity.

C10.4: 4

➤ Puppets can be used to address difficult situations that children may be experiencing. The characters can safely admit to their fears or concerns and solutions can be suggested.

C10.4: 9, 11

➤ **C10.4**: 10 · · · · · · ·

➤ **C10.4**: range 2c, · · cross-reference to **M7**

➤ **10.4**: 3 · · · · · · · ·

➤ **C10.4**: 6 · · · · · · · ·

➤ **C10.4**: 11 · · · · · ·

Puppets could be geometrical shapes like triangles for mountains, crescent moons, two triangles for a star or circles for the sun. Challenge older children to create characters from a story, such as Goldilocks or one of the Three Bears.

Evaluation

Were the children able to follow your instructions? Did you allow the children as much choice as possible? Could they think in the abstract form necessary to see only the outline of the shape? Could they create a story or situation using their puppet? Did they enjoy the 'magic' of the light show?

Supporting activity

➤ Use the 'Rangoli patterns' photocopiable sheet on page 141 to create cultural border patterns that the children can colour in and cut out to decorate the theatre frame. Use ethnic materials, such as an old sari, to drape around the shadow theatre.

Case study

Flora's mother, Ms Smith, shows her annoyance when Flora presents her with a creation of cardboard boxes, glued together and painted green. She asks what it is and Flora tells her that it is a 'green thing'. Ms Smith is unhappy and wants to know why Flora does not bring home something recognisable like the other children at your setting do. How will you respond to Ms Smith? Write down the case study with your responses for your portfolio.

Follow on

Plan different ways of presenting creative art, to give children maximum opportunities to express themselves.

Questions

(See answer pointers at end of chapter.)

10. *What considerations do you need to make when providing activities to develop imagination and creativity for children with a) visual impairment, b) cerebral palsy, and c) behavioural difficulties?*

11. *How can you make imaginative and creative activities more enjoyable, with the minimum of distractions?*

12. *Suggest opportunities to encourage non-stereotypical role-play.*

Record the questions and your full answers and share these with your assessor.

Did you know?

Many towns and cities have play resources recycling centres. Clean, safe, interesting factory waste is collected together in a centre. For a small fee, groups can collect materials to use with their children. This may include fabric, card, ribbon, balloons, buttons and sponge pieces, depending on the commercial enterprises in the area.

C10.4: 2

Extra idea

➤ At a quiet time, invite the children to listen to different types of music playing softly. In a calm voice, make suggestions that link the music to the children's experiences, such as water flowing or the wind blowing through the trees. Encourage the children to make their own suggestions.

C10.4: *cross-reference* ◄ *to* **C2**

Practical ways of collecting evidence

In addition to preparing specific activities, you should also collect evidence of sensory experiences and intellectual development during other sessions. Each time you plan an activity, assess whether there will be opportunities for gathering evidence for this Unit. Try to plan for more than one Unit at a time, for example, the activity for **C7.1** in this book can also supply evidence for **C10.4** if properly thought through.

> ### Check your progress
>
> To complete this Unit you will need to have been directly observed by your assessor for at least one aspect of each range statement in each of the four Elements. Your assessor may not see all the performance criteria, so you may have to collect this evidence by other means. Other evidence can be collected by reflective accounts of your work and witness testimonies by your colleagues.

Answer pointers

Ensure your answers are fully made for your assessor.

1. Jigsaws. Painting. Crafts. Sound bingo. Circle time. Construction toys. Retrospective activities, such as drawing, the day after a farm visit.

2. Help children: plan; learn; remember events; anticipate; think about; preparation.

3. Praise. Encourage. Give assistance. Know the child. Opportunity. Routine.

4. Weather. Plants. Pets or animals. Aircraft. Birds. Clothes. Street sounds.

5. Name senses. Sweet and sour. Tactile. Tongue. Pupil. Ear drum. Descriptive.

6. Activity centres. Music. Feely box. Party. Sand. Instruments. Tasting. Water.

7. Same and different. Above and below. First and last. Inside and outside. Back and front. Under and over. On top and underneath.

8. Keep an interest box. Worksheets. Listen to children. Suggested activities.

9. Large print. Clear illustrations. Tactile. Bright colours. Give time. Assistance. Logical progression.

10. Use child's interests. Bright colours. Aids, such as pencil grips. Staffing ratio. Lights. Computers.

11. Positioning. Quiet area. Exciting resources. Time management. Planning.

12. Dress up. Role-play area. Share experiences. Non-fiction books.

Further information

A Place to Learn by Penny Cartwright, Kym Scott and Judith Stevens (Lewisham Early Years Advice and Resource Network, 2002)

CII Promote children's language and communication development

This Unit promotes language development and communication abilities in the early years. It relates to communication between children and communication with adults, through speaking, listening, expression and understanding.

This chapter will enable you to:
C11.1 Identify stages of children's language and communication development
C11.2 Provide activities, equipment and materials to extend and reinforce children's language and communication development
C11.3 Share books, stories and rhymes to expand children's language and communication development
C11.4 Provide communication opportunities to enhance and reinforce children's language and communication development
C11.5 Interact with children to promote their language and communication development.

Element CII.I Identify stages of children's language and communication development

Your assessor can observe and question you.

My special book

➤ *C11.1: range 1 · · · ·*   *Number of children: one-to-one, or with a small group.*   ◄

Resources
Two sheets of stiff A4 card per child; paper; treasury tags; stapler; glue; hole-punch; mark-making, painting or flat collage materials; disposable or Polaroid camera; photographs of the children, their family and the setting.

Preparation
Plan the activity using the 'Activity plan' photocopiable sheet on page 131. Ask parents to bring in family photographs, one from every year of their child's life, if possible.

What to do
➤ Invite the children to take photographs of their favourite toy or friend.

➤ Encourage the children to assemble their own books with help.

➤ Suggest that the children begin with their names, birthdays and age.

➤ Over a period of time encourage the children to add self-portraits, pictures of their family, photographs, artwork and items significant to them.

➤ Intersperse the children's work with stories they have told you, thoughtful statements they have made and records of significant events.

➤ Help the children to punch holes in the pages and fix them in sequence with treasury tags between the card covers. Let them decorate the cover.

➤ Use these books to discuss, recall memories and look at sequencing.

Tip

➤ It is important to show that all languages are equally respected.

C11.1: 6

Support and extension

Assist younger children to take photographs. Suggest comments, but only use if agreed. Invite older children to add emergent writing or stories.

Evaluation

Did the children progress their books at their own pace? Are their skills and knowledge developing? Are all the books different? Did the children make their own choices? Did you gain permission from the parents to take photographs?

Supporting activity

Make a long-term child study, taking particular note of language and communication skills. Note interaction between child and parent, child and child, and child and practitioner. Record details of verbal and non-verbal communication. This is helpful if the child has communication difficulties, as you can identify the stage of development in order to give support.

Case study

➤ Xavier is two and will start at your setting in a month. He was born with a cleft lip and palate, which has been repaired. How might this affect his speech and language development? How will you prepare for him? Write down the case study with your responses for your portfolio.

C11.1: 4, 5, range 1b, ◄
2a, b

Follow on

Find out about four health professionals who are involved with your setting, including speech therapists. Where can you find them? What is their role? What is your role? Find out what sources of information about development and care are available to you. Discuss with your assessor.

Questions

(See answer pointers at end of chapter.)

➤ **1.** *How do find out that children have receptive language? What are the signs?*   **C11.1**: 1, 2, 3 ◄

➤ **2.** *Name the barriers to children's language and communication development.*   **C11.1**: 4 ◄

➤ **3.** *What are the stages of development of language and communication in* · · · **C11.1**: 6 ◄
children who have more than one language?

Record the questions and your full answers and share these with your assessor.

Did you know?

Research shows that the way adults talk to babies has a distinctive vowel sound that characterises baby talk. The vowel sounds are phonetically different than when speaking to adults and are clearer. Whichever country people come from they seem to naturally adopt this speech pattern.

C11.1: 1

Extra idea

➤ *C11.1: 3* · · · · · · · · Over a period of time, record a child's language to show their development. ◄
This can be shared with the parents and passed on when they move to a new setting. Record on the 'Development chart' photocopiable sheet on page 142.

Element C11.2 Provide activities, equipment and materials to extend and reinforce children's language and communication development

➤ *C11.2: range 1d,* · · · Your assessor can observe and question you.   ◄
3a, b, c, d, 4c

Sand tray interests
Number of children: four.

Resources
Individual sand trays; silver sand; assorted small-world toys including people, farm animals, wild animals and dinosaurs; natural materials, such as twigs, leaves, rocks, shells and fir cones; toy cars; tractors; plastic fish; teaset; food colouring; jug of water; wooden beads; thick and thin cardboard; glue.

Preparation
Plan the activity using the 'Activity plan' photocopiable sheet on page 131. Place the sand trays and resources in an area where relevant posters and displays relating to the subjects chosen can easily be seen.

What to do
➤ Plan the session as a group. Different ideas are suggested below.
➤ Invite the children to add food colouring to the water and then mix it with the sand.
➤ Suggest the children create a forest with twigs, leaves and fir cones and add animals.
➤ Let the children make cardboard houses and add small-world people.
➤ Help the children make under-water scenes with rocks and shells.
➤ Show the children how to use their fingers to trace out letters or words.
➤ Fix safe and definable objects on a board, such as small toys, a plastic plate, a beaker or a string of wooden beads. Hide the board at the bottom of the sand tray and ask the children to identify the items by touch. Make a variety of different boards.

✔ **Tip**
➤ Silver sand is preferable for children to play in, as builders sand is red and stains badly unless bought as twice-washed sand.

Support and extension

Allow younger children to explore the sand and tell you what they feel.
Challenge older children to create a story and take turns to develop it.

Evaluation

➤ Make a note of which activities were most popular. Were any unsafe? Can
you suggest other attractions to increase the value of sand play and reinforce
language development? Did you observe and record the verbal exchanges?

Cross-reference to ◄
C16

Supporting activity

Use alternative mediums, such as sterilised coconut fibre. Place the fibre on a
plastic sheet, add animals and natural materials to create a textured jungle.

Case study

➤ Tala is three and a half and has always been more practical than
communicative, although she can speak when she wants to. She enjoys
practical activities, often seeming too busy to talk. What activities and
materials can you offer to reinforce her language learning and encourage
her to communicate with other children and practitioners? Write down
the case study with your responses for your portfolio.

C11.2: 1 ◄

Follow on

➤ Consider how a baby's language is reinforced by repetition, interpretation
and encouragement. How can this approach be developed in a reluctant
three-year-old speaker? Imagine a scenario and discuss with your
assessor.

C11.2: 6 ◄

Questions

(See answer pointers at end of chapter.)

➤ **4.** *What activities can you suggest to encourage communication turn-taking?* · · **C11.2**: 1 ◄

➤ **5.** *What strategies can you use to ensure your activities and equipment offer* · · **C11.2**: 2 ◄
anti-discriminatory play and opportunities for language development?

➤ **6.** *Can you categorise the ways we use language? Give examples of each* · · · · **C11.2**: 3 ◄
category from your own experience.

Record the questions and your full answers and share these with your assessor.

Did you know?

It is estimated that there are over 140 languages spoken in inner
London alone. It is not unusual to have 30 different languages spoken
in one setting.

Extra idea

➤ Copy the photocopiable 'Spider chart' on page 132. Write 'Play for · · · · · · **C11.2**: 1, 2, 3, 4, 6, 7 ◄
reinforcing children's language' in the centre. Add suggestions in the
surrounding boxes. Explain how language and communication can be
developed using each suggestion. Keep a record of this in your portfolio.

Element C11.3 Share books, stories and rhymes to expand children's language and communication development

➤ **C11.3**: *range 1a,* · · · Your assessor can observe and question you.
b, c

Action book corner
This is an exciting project to get children actively involved in books for
information and books for the imagination.
Number of children: four.

Resources
Book corner with shelving; theme-related books, articles, posters and, if
possible, furniture, such as drapes for the entrance and laminated notices.

Preparation
Plan the activity using the 'Activity plan' photocopiable sheet on page 131.
Involve the children in the planning and use their ideas where practical. Invite
parents to bring in items from home or to become involved in setting up the
book corner.

What to do
➤ Decide on the theme and set up the action book corner.
➤ For example, for the theme of 'Feasts' you can create a kitchen with
books, a checked tablecloth on a table with chairs around, checked aprons for
the children, a cardboard door with the word 'Kitchen' on it, and pictures of
food and feasts from different cultures on the wall at child height.
➤ Encourage the children to discuss the theme and suggest ways to develop

it. For example, ask the children to suggest food for a
feast, write the recipe out and make the dish
together as a group. Organise a feast within the
setting with the parents actively involved in the
associated activities.
➤ With other themes, use tunnels or saris as curtains
for the children to enter the area through. Patterned
curtains, sheeting, netting, bead curtains and strands of
yarn or ribbons, all make exciting entrances.
➤ Expand the theme into group story time, circle
time, visits and visitors, making theme books and
activities both indoors and outdoors.

Support and extension
Remind younger children about the links between
the theme and the books. Keep activities simple and
be on hand to assist when necessary. Encourage
older children to share their own theme-related
experiences with the group.

early years
training &
management

Evaluation

Did the children respond to the chosen theme? Did you choose the books carefully to avoid stereotyping and discrimination? Were you able to extend the children's language, introduce new ideas and call on their experience? What can you do differently? What other themes can you introduce?

Supporting activity

Sometimes children with medical conditions or disabilities will miss out on play experiences due to regular absences from the setting. However, they often have a range of experiences and language that other children may not. Use these different experiences to both boost the children's self-esteem and inform their peers.

> **✓ Tip**
>
> ➤ Children can have their own library book as soon as they have a name. Encourage parents to join up on their baby's behalf.
>
> *C11.3*: 7

Case study

➤ Mickey is three years old. He has never been confident and now, as his mother is due to give birth to a new baby, he has become clingy and distressed. How can you support him through what is obviously a difficult time? How can you develop his knowledge and understanding of the situation? Write down the case study with your responses for your portfolio.

C11.3: 2, 7 ◄

Follow on

➤ Categorise the setting's books in groups, such as non-fiction, fiction, situational, dual language, picture books, reading books and story-books for adults to read to their child. Write an assessment of your findings, where the strengths and gaps are, and place in your portfolio. Share your findings with your assessor.

C11.3: 1 ◄

Questions

(See answer pointers at end of chapter.)

➤ **7.** *When selecting books for young children, what type of pictures should you · · look for? What makes a good book?*   *C11.3*: 2 ◄

➤ **8.** *How can you encourage children to actively participate when sharing stories?*   *C11.3*: 6 ◄

➤ **9.** *What is the difference between telling a story and reading a story?* · · · · · ·   *C11.3*: 7 ◄

Record the questions and your full answers and share these with your assessor.

Did you know?

Book Start is a UK-wide initiative to give babies two free books at their seven- to nine-month health check and to supply parents with advice via their Health Visitor. More than one million babies have benefited from the scheme, which encourages parents and carers to share books with their babies. For more information visit: www.bookstart.co.uk

Extra idea

➤ Use a variety of props and aids for storytelling. These could include hats, · · · ·   *C11.3*: 6, 7 ◄
puppets, pictures, scarves and toys from the setting.

Element C11.4 Provide communication opportunities to enhance and reinforce children's language and communication development

➤ **C11.4**: *range 1a,* · · · Your assessor can observe and question you.   ◄
b, c, d

Listening games
Number of children: six, or whole group.

Resources
Commercial or home-made 'Sound lotto' games consisting of a tape recording of familiar sounds children will recognise, with matching pictures or objects; tape recorder; selection of bells, such as bicycle bell, doorbell, cat bell, percussion bell, school bell and dancing bells; musical instruments.

Preparation
Plan the activity using the 'Activity plan' photocopiable sheet on page 131.

What to do
➤ At circle time, encourage the children to listen to the sounds outside. Ask the children what they can hear, what they think is happening and where they have heard the sounds before. Discuss the responses as a group.
➤ Explain the rules of 'Sound lotto'. Give the children a set of sound images each, invite them to listen to the recorded sounds and match the sounds to their pictures. Stop the tape after each sound and discuss with the children.
➤ Lay the bells out on a table so that the children can clearly see them all. Play a recording of one of the bells and ask the children to identify the correct bell. As a group, discuss the differences in the sounds and invite the children to suggest when and where they would be used.
➤ Remember to listen to the children, so they learn to listen to others.

> **✓ Tip**
> ➤ Reinforce the importance of language by encouraging children to take and receive messages in the setting.
>
> C11.4: 3

Support and extension
Use fewer, more distinctive sounds with younger children and children for whom English is an additional language. Play 'Chinese whispers' with older children.

Evaluation
How effective was the activity? Did it stimulate discussion, involving listening and responding? Were the recorded sounds clear or indistinct out of context? Are there other ways of doing the activity? Can you suggest another activity to reinforce children's language and communication development?

Supporting activity
➤ **C11.4**: 2 · · · · · · · Give the children a prop or musical instrument each, to introduce at a   ◄
particular point in a story. Ask the children to listen carefully to the story and make their contribution every time their prompt is made.

Case study

➤ As an only child, Jade spends most of her time with adults. Her language seems very mature and she often finds it difficult to communicate with her peers. How can you help Jade communicate more effectively in your group and make friends? How can Jade enhance the communication skills of her peers? Write down the case study with your responses for your portfolio.

C11.4: 4 ◄

Follow on

➤ Make a list of the children's interests. Devise ways of using these ideas to enhance and reinforce language and communication development.

C11.4: 5 ◄

Questions

(See answer pointers at end of chapter.)

➤ **10.** *What spontaneous opportunities may occur to engage children in* · · : · · · · *C11.4: 1, 2* ◄
conversation, listening and turn-taking?

➤ **11.** *Suggest ways to reinforce language and introduce new words.* · · · · · · · · *C11.4: 7* ◄

➤ **12.** *What is meant by 'open-ended' and 'closed' questions? Give examples of* · · *C11.4: 9* ◄
how you would use both.

Record the questions and your full answers and share these with your assessor.

Did you know?

Babies learn the skill of turn-taking during the pre-verbal or 'babbling' stage. They listen and respond by babbling. If two adults are talking, the baby turns from one to the other, to look at whoever is speaking. This reinforces the concept that talking involves taking turns to speak.

C11.4: 2

Extra idea

➤ Use the 'Picture sequence' photocopiable sheet on page 143 to help children order events. Copy the sheet for the children to cut out and rearrange. Let the children decide the order of the story, develop the story using picture clues and reinforce and enhance the language used.

C11.4: 5, 6, 7, 8 ◄

Element C11.5 Interact with children to promote their language and communication development

➤ Your assessor can observe and question you. · *C11.5: range 1a, b, c,* ◄
d, 2a

Picture box

Number of children: six, or with individual children.

Resources

Cardboard box with lid, such as a shoebox; magazines; thin card; PVA glue; spreaders; glue brushes; scissors; laminator, if available.

Preparation
Plan the activity using the 'Activity plan' photocopiable sheet on page 131.

What to do
➤ Let the children choose pictures to cut out from the magazines.
➤ Invite the children to glue the pictures to pieces of card that are large enough to handle and that fit in the box.
➤ Laminate the cards or invite the children to paint with diluted PVA glue.
➤ Cover the lid and sides of the box with pictures.
➤ Ask a child to remove one card from the box, describe it and keep it.
➤ The pictures can be used to make up a story, to prompt memories, to extend language and to involve reluctant speakers.

Support and extension
Provide younger children with pre-cut pictures. Help very young children to create the cards. Add a descriptive word for older children to read.

✓ Tip

➤ Language improves when children are praised as their self-esteem is raised.

Evaluation
Did the activity stimulate discussion? Did the children think of ideas for sets of themed cards? Did you think of other ways of using the picture box? If you made another box in the future would you do it differently? If so, how?

C11.5: 6

➤ **C11.5**: 7 · · · · · · ·

Supporting activity
Stick pictures of familiar objects to six sides of a cube and use as a dice. ◄
Name and match with the real thing.

➤ **C11.5**: 5 · · · · · · ·

Case study
Three-year-old Poppy is a quiet, shy child who speaks in a whisper, ◄
finding it difficult to get close to an adult to communicate. Her brother is a year older and has a habit of moving in close and speaking loudly. How can you help both children to adjust to the setting and provide for the needs of the children? Write down the case study with your responses for your portfolio.

➤ **C11.5**: 1, 6 · · · · · ·

Follow on
Some children find it difficult to communicate as all they hear at home are ◄
barked commands and swear words. Consider ways to help these children develop the social skills to communicate effectively with their peers.

Questions
(See answer pointers at end of chapter.)

➤ **C11.5**: 3 · · · · · · · **13.** *How can you minimise the noise in a setting when communicating with* ◄
children?

➤ **C11.5**: 4 · · · · · · · **14.** *How can non-verbal communication enhance and reinforce verbal* ◄
communication?

➤ **C11.5**: 7 · · · · · · · **15.** *How can your knowledge of a child's background and personal experience* ◄
be used to promote their language development?

Record the questions and your full answers and share these with your assessor.

Did you know?

Interaction with adults and children is *the* most important aspect in acquiring language. Research shows that, in the early years, parents and practitioners provide the basis for communication on which children build their vocabulary and thinking.

C11.5: 6

Extra idea

➤ At circle time pass a small toy around the group. Explain that the children can only speak when they have the toy. This encourages turn-taking.

C11.5: 8 ◄

Practical ways of collecting evidence

Tape-record spontaneous and planned conversations with children. Let children make their own recordings, which you can evaluate as evidence.

Check your progress

To complete this Unit you will need to have been directly observed by your assessor for at least one aspect of each range statement in each of the five Elements. Much of the evidence will be collected throughout your NVQ assessment as language can be observed on every occasion. Ensure it is recorded on the direct observation sheets, when assessment is made for other Units, and cross-referenced into **C11**.

Answer pointers

Ensure your answers are fully made for your assessor.

1. Response. Carrying out instruction. Non-verbal. Progress. Sign language.

2. Stammering. Medical conditions. Hearing impairment. Cleft lip or palate.

3. Initially delayed. Mixing languages. Separating languages in context. Benefiting through expression later on.

4. Telephones. Tape recorders. Puppets. Made-up stories. Role-play. Interest tables. Displays. Plan activities with children. Ask questions.

5. Policy. Selection. Images. Adult language. Language used. Access.

6. Task. Expression. Conversation. Reconstruction. Information.

7. Non-stereotypical. Gender. Race. Culture. Clear. Attractive.

8. Puppets. Adult writing child's story. Props. Taking seriously.

9. Involve children. Make personal. Animation. Regular words. Confidence.

10. Play time. Hand-washing time. Lunch time. On visits. Travelling.

11. Story time. Developing child's ideas. Repetition. Explanation. Poetry.

12. What is...? Why do you...? What if...? Are you wet? Extending language. Child lacking confidence.

13. Quiet area. Carpet. Raise hands. Staff ratios. Turn-taking.

14. Facial expression. Body language. Eye contact. Miss words from songs.

15. Understand. Interpretation. Realistic expectations. Alternative methods.

Further information

Supporting Identity, Diversity and Language in the Early Years by Iram Siraj-Blatchford and Priscilla Clarke (Oxford University Press, 2000)

C15 Contribute to the protection of children from abuse

This Unit identifies the signs and symptoms of abuse, handling disclosures, recording and reporting possible abuse and personal safety and awareness.

This chapter will enable you to:

C15.1 Identify signs and symptoms of possible abuse
C15.2 Respond to a child's disclosure of abuse
C15.3 Inform other professionals about suspected abuse
C15.4 Promote children's awareness of personal safety and abuse.

Element C15.1 Identify signs and symptoms of possible abuse

Child-related activities are not appropriate in this Element. Children need to be aware of body issues and this activity is related to **C15.4**: range 1a, b, c, 2a, b, c, d. Your assessor can observe you with the children to provide evidence for **C15.4**, question you on the thinking behind this activity and question you on any other evidence presented for **C15.1**.

Body popper
Number of children: six.

Tip
➤ Without being intrusive, a child can be observed when changing for PE.

C15.1: *1*

➤ Any concerns, no matter how trivial they may seem at the time, *must* be reported to someone in authority. Other information may be known of which you are unaware. Always record unusual behaviour or suspicious injury.

C15.1: *3, 4*

Resources
Card suitable for photocopier; crayons or felt tips; scissors.

Preparation
Plan the activity using the 'Activity plan' photocopiable sheet on page 131. Copy the 'Body popping' photocopiable sheet on page 144 for each child.

What to do
➤ Discuss with the children the different parts of the body that are named on the photocopiable sheet.
➤ Discuss the importance of keeping their bodies safe from harm.
➤ Assure the children that it is their body and to tell a trusted adult if they do not like what someone is doing to them.
➤ Talk about the rules of your setting, such as not bullying or teasing.
➤ Ask the children to colour in the body parts as they name them.

Support and extension

Keep the discussion simple with younger children and help them to cut around the shapes. Teach older children about more body parts, such as chins, elbows, ankles and eyebrows.

Evaluation

How familiar were the children with the body parts named? Record your findings and discuss with colleagues. How else can you use the photocopiable sheet? Did a discussion on personal safety develop? Will you use the sheet again with the same age group?

Supporting activities

➤ Cut the 'Body popping' sheet into named parts and use as a jigsaw puzzle.
➤ Ask the children to look in a mirror and paint a self-portrait.

Case study

➤ Chandler's mum has recently started potty training him, as she is having difficulty with the washing and the cost of nappies. She is 16 and is largely unsupported. Chandler is normally a happy child, but has recently become withdrawn and gets distressed if taken to the toilet. When changing his wet pants you notice he has a ring of bruises on his buttocks. What do you think has caused these? What will you do about it and what can be done in the situation? Write down the case study with your responses for your portfolio.

C15.1: 1, 3, 4, 5, 6, 7, 8 ◄

Follow on

➤ Look at issues facing young parents, such as housing, poverty, support, parenting, isolation and education, and how practitioners can support them with these problems.

C15.1: 6 ◄

Questions

(See answer pointers at end of chapter.)

➤ **1.** *What is confidentiality and why is it important to maintain it in your setting?* *C15.1*: 5 ◄

➤ **2.** *Who is involved in child protection if suspicions are raised in your setting?* · · *C15.1*: 6 ◄

➤ **3.** *Suggest signs and symptoms that may make you suspect potential abuse.* · · *C15.1*: 7 ◄

Record the questions and your full answers and share these with your assessor.

Did you know?

Ninety per cent of African-Caribbean babies have a bluish-grey birthmark, mostly over the back and buttocks, called a Mongolian spot. They vary in size, and most fade away by two or three years. They can be mistaken for abuse.

C15.1: 6

Extra idea

Consider reflective accounts, witness testimonies, diary records, reports, records and child observations, as it is not easy to make direct observations for this Unit.

Element C15.2 Respond to a child's disclosure of abuse

➤ **C15.2**: *range 1a,* · · · · Your assessor can observe and question you.   ◄
b, c, d

Listening opportunities
Number of children: one-to-one and small groups.

Resources
Appropriate to the chosen activity.

Preparation
Plan the activity using the 'Activity plan' photocopiable sheet on page 131.
Prepare the appropriate resources according to activity.

Tip

➤ If children make a
personal disclosure, they need
to know they are believed,
they are respected, it is not
their fault, that what they
have done in disclosing is
right and action will be taken.

C15.2: 2

➤ If your setting has a form
to record disclosure or
suspected abuse, fill in a blank
copy according to an
imaginary situation. Make it
clear on the form that this is
an invented situation and
cannot be traced back to a
particular child.

C15.2: 6

➤ *Cross-reference to* · · ·
C11 and C16

➤ **C15.2**: *1, 2, 3, 4,* · · ·
5, 6, 7

What to do
➤ Keeping open the lines of communication between child and adult is
important in being receptive to messages about abuse.
➤ Read stories that raise relevant issues. Give the characters a positive
outcome because they shared their concerns with someone else.
➤ Use puppets to open a child up to 'talk' about issues through a character.
➤ Role-play gives children the freedom to act out issues and resolutions.
Verbal and non-verbal communication suggest areas for further investigation.
➤ Ask open-ended questions to which the child has to give a thoughtful
answer. Listen carefully. It is inappropriate to ask direct or probing questions.
➤ Small-world play in a dolls' house gives children the opportunity to act out
domestic scenes in a safe manner.

Support and extension
Language used must be appropriate to the age of the child. Use and expect
simpler information with younger children.

Evaluation
Did the children have opportunities to express themselves? Can you think of
other opportunities for listening to children's conversations and expressions?

Supporting activity
Observe children freely expressing their thoughts and concerns. Record your   ◄
findings at several different points over a period of time.

Case study
Seven-year-old Emily used to chat about everything, but is now quiet and   ◄
often found on her own in the corner of the library rather than with her
peers, shying away from the male member of staff. How can you
encourage her to share her concerns? What will you do with any
information if it relates to potential child abuse? Write down the case
study with your responses for your portfolio.

Follow on

Find out how child abuse is viewed in different cultures. Smacking and female circumcision are important to consider. Would you approach the disclosure of these actions in the same way as neglect or sexual abuse? Discuss with your colleagues and share your findings with your assessor.

Questions

(See answer pointers at end of chapter.)

➤ **4.** *Who is responsible for ensuring cases of potential child abuse are acted upon in your setting? Who else needs to be informed?*   **C15.2**: 3   ◀

➤ **5.** *Confidentiality is considered sacrosanct in most situations. Why is it different in the case of a child disclosing potential abuse?*   **C15.2**: 4   ◀

➤ **6.** *How would you feel if you reported a disclosure of abuse a child had made · · to you, and where would you expect to get emotional support for yourself?*   **C15.2**: 7   ◀

Record the questions and your full answers and share these with your assessor.

Did you know?

It is understood that more than 90 per cent of adult communication is non-verbal. According to David McNeill, Professor of Psychology and Linguistics at Chicago University, 'To study language by listening only to utterances is to miss as much as 75 per cent of the meaning'.

C15.2: 5

Extra idea

➤ If a disclosure is made to you, follow the procedure of the setting and ask the relevant individual to write a witness testimony confirming your actions.   **C15.2**: 1, 3, 6   ◀

Element C15.3 Inform other professionals about suspected abuse

Child-related activities are not appropriate in this Element. Children can be made aware of issues of personal safety and this activity is related to **C15.4**: range 1a, b, c, 2a, b, c. Your assessor can observe you with the children to provide evidence for **C15.4**, question you on the thinking behind this activity and on any other evidence presented for **C15.3**.

The safety game

Number of children: four, or can be used on a one-to-one basis.

Resources

'Safety game' photocopiable sheet on page 145; thin card; scissors; glue; laminator, if available.

Preparation

Plan the activity using the 'Activity plan' photocopiable sheet on page 131. Make three copies of the 'Safety game' sheet on to thin card, cut out cards and mount.

> Never use a child's real name or identification details when submitting work in a portfolio.

What to do

> You will need to stimulate discussion, and support and reassure the children.
> Show the children the cards and explain the issues to them.
> Stack the cards face down in the centre of the table.
> Invite a child to remove the top card and identify the message. Support the children while they become familiar with the images.
> Use the card to explain what is meant by strangers, bad secrets, who to trust and what the message means.
> Allow all the children time to express their views, fears and experiences.
> Use the game cards to explore difficult issues raised after the activity.
> Reassure the children that they will be safe if they follow the messages.

Support and extension

> *Cross-reference to · · ·*
> *C11*

Keep the messages very simple with younger children. Extend the activity into role-playing the actions with older children to reinforce the message.

Evaluation

Were you able to raise issues without fear? Were questions raised that you found difficult to answer? Do you need to find out more about child abuse or how to discuss it with children? Can you think of other ways to use the cards?

Supporting activity

> *C15.3*: 2, 6 · · · · · ·

Find out about different types of child abuse, its impact on the child, child protection and the confidentiality policies in your setting. Consider the impact on the abuser and the family, if action is taken, and how all parties can be supported in the interest of the child.

> *C15.3*: 1, 2, 3, 4, · · ·
> 5, 6

Case study

On Monday morning two-year-old Jacob is brought in by his mother, saying, 'You have him, I've had enough'. She rushes away. Jacob is still in his filthy pyjamas and the same nappy he went home in on Friday evening. He is quiet and withdrawn. His only action is to snatch a piece of toast from your hand to eat. What will you do? Who needs to know? What information will they need? What will they do with that information? What will the consequences be? Write down the case study with your responses for your portfolio.

Follow on

> *C15.3*: 1, 6 · · · · · ·

Find out what is meant by the boundaries of confidentiality, who you can share information with, where information is stored and what details you can put in your portfolio. Write a short confidentiality policy for your portfolio.

Questions

(See answer pointers at end of chapter.)

> *C15.3*: 2, 4, 5 · · · · · ·

7. *What is the value of routine observations and record keeping in the identification of potential child abuse?*

> *C15.3*: 3 · · · · · · · ·

8. *How soon should possible abuse be reported?*

➤ **9.** *How can you decide what is relevant information in relation to potential* · · · **C15.3**: 4 ◀
child abuse? Include direct information, indirect information and rumour.

Record the questions and your full answers and share these with your assessor.

Did you know?
Article 19 of the United Nations Convention on the Rights of the Child
is in two parts and states:

1. Parties shall take all appropriate legislative, administrative, social
and educational measures to protect the child from all forms of
physical or mental violence, injury or abuse, neglect or negligent
treatment, malnutrition or exploitation including sexual abuse, while in
the care of parent(s), legal guardian(s), or any other person who has
the care of the child.

2. Such protective measures should, as appropriate, include effective
procedures for the establishment of social programmes to provide
necessary support for the child and for those who have the care of the
child, as well as for other forms of prevention and for identification,
reporting, referral, investigation, treatment, and follow-up of instances
of child maltreatment.

Extra idea
➤ Copy the 'Spider chart' photocopiable sheet on page 132. Write 'Relevant · · **C15.3**: 5 ◀
individuals in child abuse procedures' in the centre and add the titles or roles
of relevant people in the surrounding boxes.

Element C15.4 Promote children's awareness of personal safety and abuse

➤ Your assessor can observe and question you. · · · · · · · · · · · · · · **C15.4**: *range 1a b, c,* ◀
2a, b, c

I'm number one
The following are suggestions for a theme to build
up the children's awareness of their own bodies,
personal safety and protection from abuse. Use
the activities to stimulate discussion about their
bodies and themselves. Other activities for this
Element can be found in sections **C15.1** and
C15.3 in this book.
Number of children: six.

Resources
Appropriate to the chosen activity.

Preparation
Plan the activity using the 'Activity plan'
photocopiable sheet on page 131.

> Awareness of personal safety and abuse should be introduced as part of the regular routine.

C15.4: 1

What to do

➤ Cut out strips of skin tone coloured paper, to the children's exact heights. Fix to the wall. Attach photos of the children to the top. Let the children create hand and feet prints to fix to the bottom and part way up. Use these images as a point of reference for similarities and differences.

➤ Use commercial jigsaw puzzles, posters and photo cards to stimulate discussion with the children about our bodies and ourselves.

➤ Print digital photos of the group on card and make into a jigsaw puzzle.

➤ Play the 'What if?' game. Practise questions with the children, such as 'What if someone cuddles you and you did not like it?' and 'What if you are being bullied?'. Teach the children to shout if they are frightened.

Support and extension

Ensure that the activities are appropriate to the age of the children.

Evaluation

Did the activities help the children take pride in their bodies and teach them to say no if they are not happy? Can you think of other relevant activities?

Supporting activity

Visit the website: www.kidscape.org.uk for information on child protection.

➤ **C15.4: 4** · · · · · · ·

Case study

After watching the boys, three-year-old Carrie tried standing up to use the toilet. She was distressed as she wet herself. How will you deal with the situation? Write down the case study with your responses for your portfolio.

Follow on

It is common for children to become distressed at the arrival of new siblings. What will you consider when discussing these issues with children?

Questions

(See answer pointers at end of chapter.)

➤ **C15.4: 6** · · · · · · · · **10.** *How can you encourage children to assert their rights?*

➤ **C15.4: 7** · · · · · · · · **11.** *What does personal safety mean for a child?*

➤ **C15.4: 8** · · · · · · · · **12.** *How can you encourage children to express fears, anxieties and feelings?*

Record the questions and your full answers and share these with your assessor.

Did you know?

The Department of Health document, *Working Together to Safeguard Children* (1999), states, 'Cultural factors neither explain nor condone acts of omission or commission which place a child at risk of significant harm. Professionals should be aware of the work with the strengths and support systems available within families, ethnic groups and communities, which can build upon and help safeguard children and promote their welfare'.

Extra idea

➤ Look for anatomically correct toys and images in early years catalogues. · · · · **C15.4**: 4 ◄

Practical ways of collecting evidence

➤ Children often have bumps and bruises as part of their normal play. To · · · · **C15.1**: 4, cross-
establish the potential for these injuries observe children, at different times, *reference to* **C16** ◄
during active play. Note when you see children in a situation that could result
in injury. Record any injuries and potential injuries, and where it may occur on
the body. When learning about physical abuse and suspicious injuries, you will
have an idea of what is a normal level of injury to compare against.

> ### Check your progress
> Much of the evidence for this Unit will be by methods other than direct
> observation by your assessor. Assessment will rely on witness
> testimonies, reflective accounts, incident reports seen by your assessor,
> diaries, plans for activities, questioning and child observations.

Answer pointers

Ensure your answers are fully made for your assessor.
1. Authority. Confidence. Trust. Not gossiping. Protection. Respect.
2. Senior staff. Health Visitor. Parents. Doctor. Social Worker. Designated
teacher. Child psychologist. OFSTED.
3. Finger-tip bruising. Regression. Withdrawal. Differing stories. Several small
round burns. Soreness of anus or vulva. Dip scalds. Soft tissue bruising.
4. Designated person. Policy. Police. NSPCC. Senior colleague. Social Worker.
5. Promises not made. Cannot be ignored. Advice sought. Policy.
6. Upset. Frightened. Nervous. Sick. Angry. Senior colleagues. NSPCC.
7. Evidence. Ongoing records. Written. Dated. Patterns. Injuries.
8. Without delay. When requested.
9. Direct observation. Differing accounts. Informed by reliable witnesses.
Circumstantial evidence. Check sources. Record type of evidence.
10. Confidence. Decision-making. Choice. Say no. Assertive. Give support.
11. Get out of harmful situations. Know good from bad. Trust. Stranger
danger.
12. Reassure. Share. Verbal encouragement. Listen. Take seriously.

Further information

Keeping Safe: A Practical Guide to Talking with Children by Michele Elliot
(Hodder and Stoughton, 1994)

Working Together to Safeguard Children (Department of Health, 1999)

C16 Observe and assess the development and behaviour of children

This Unit covers observations of children, individually and in a group, and are used for assessment, planning, recording progress and for children with special needs statementing. Various observational methods are addressed.

This chapter will enable you to:
C16.1 Observe children's behaviour and performance
C16.2 Use observation results to inform the children's future care and education.

Element C16.1 Observe children's behaviour and performance

➤ *C3.1*: 1 · · · · · · · · Observation of children is not an area where you are expected to be directly ◄ observed by your assessor. The suggestions made are to enable you to plan the play area with a view to observing children at a range of activities.

Play for observation
Number of children: whole group for planning, small groups for activities.

Resources
A4 paper; pen; 'Spider chart' photocopiable sheet on page 132; appropriate resources for chosen activity.

Preparation
In the centre of the 'Spider chart' write 'Observation opportunities'. In the surrounding boxes suggest types of play, the activity and the method of observation you intend using. Draw up a plan of the room on the A4 sheet of paper, indicating where you would place equipment. This can be a real or an imaginary play area. Plan to undertake observations over a period of weeks.

What to do
➤ Record observations in various ways, such as written narrative form, a tick sheet, over different times, for a specific purpose or as a general developmental record. Decide which method is most appropriate. You need to show you have used various methods, evaluated the records and can demonstrate how you will put that knowledge into the planning process.

early years
training & management

Methods of recording observations

♦ **Descriptive** – This written record describes all you are seeing happening and is written in the present tense. It needs practice to note all the things you are seeing, but requires no special forms only a notebook and pen.

♦ **Tick sheet** – See the 'Observational tick chart' photocopiable sheet on page 146. Add headings for the areas you observe, either with an individual or a group. When you see the activity add a tick and add up afterwards.

♦ **Target child** – This is a focused approach for an individual child, perhaps to explain when and why a particular behaviour occurs. Observe when the behaviour is likely to occur, to identify the triggers, such as unwanted behaviour, or to identify strengths, or areas needing support.

♦ **Event sample** – Observe a child or a group for a given amount of time throughout a session, such as one minute in every ten, to give a flavour of what is happening throughout the day. This is also called time sampling.

♦ **Tracking chart** – Draw a diagram of the play area, indicating the different activities. Note the movements of a child between activities using arrows, noting how long is spent at each activity. You may find that some equipment is never used, so try moving it and observe again.

➤ You need to set out a reason for each observation, such as, finding out the most used equipment or what triggers a child's anti-social behaviour. The following are examples, but you may wish to choose alternative techniques.

➤ Ask the children to draw their favourite vegetables on A5 paper to make a group display of harvest time. Observe the children drawing and record their conversation using the descriptive method, writing down all you see and hear happening. Ask the children to cut out the picture, mount on brown sugar paper, shaped as a basket, and display. Evaluate your results to assess fine motor skills, language development, social skills and food awareness.

➤ Copy the 'Observation tick chart' photocopiable sheet on page 146 to use during active play. See the completed 'Observation tick chart' (right), showing how to fill the form in. For example, in observing the gender differences in types of play, you can ask, 'Do boys really play on the bikes more than girls?', 'Are the girls more likely to play with other girls?' and, 'If given the same equipment, do boys and girls use it differently?'. Write the activities you will observe at the side of the chart and the behaviour you will test across the top. Make several recordings over a given time, for example, every five minutes for a 15-minute period. You can put several ticks in each box or copy the sheet once the headings are filled in for use over a longer time scale.

➤ Alternatively you may wish to observe a snapshot of what play the children are involved in at a particular point. Write the children's names down the side of the chart and the range of activities across the

Tip

➤ Ask for the children's permission to observe them.

C16.1: 2

➤ Confidentiality must be maintained according to the policies of the setting. If you need to identify unfamiliar children give them stickers and use this as the identification rather than by name.

C16.1: 9

Cross-reference to C2, ◄
C3, C5, C11

Photocopiable

Observation tick chart

Child(ren): Nursery / Age(s): 3-4		Fast	Slow	Aggressive/Crashing	Solitary	With others	Quiet play	Noisy play	Playing with others same gender	Playing with others opposite gender
Bikes	Boys	✓✓	✓	✓✓		✓✓/✓			✓✓/✓	✓✓
Bikes	Girls		✓			✓	✓✓		✓✓/✓	
Football	Boys					✓✓/✓			✓✓/✓	
Football	Girls					✓			✓	
Other ball games	Boys				✓✓	✓✓			✓	✓
Other ball games	Girls					✓	✓✓			✓
Skipping	Boys					✓			✓	
Skipping	Girls					✓✓/✓			✓✓/✓	
Running	Boys					✓✓/✓			✓✓/✓	✓✓
Running	Girls					✓✓			✓✓	

Date: 9.8.02   Observation time scale: 10.15 - 10.30/Every 5 minutes

Subject: Gender differences in active play

Observer: Meg Jones

PHOTOCOPIABLE

(146) ■SCHOLASTIC   Gaining your NVQ level 3 early years training & management

Event sampling chart

Time	Activity	Who with	Language	Comment
9.15am	Pattern making -fingerprints	Practitioner A	None	Focusing on activity
9.20	Fingerprints covering page	Joined by Sara	'I can do that'	Said by Sara and directed to Ade
9.25	Painting hands	Jessie and Kate join in	Kate to Jessie 'you help me'	Ade ignoring other children
9.30	Returning to play area	Joined by Laurie	'Come and see my car'	Offer made to Ade
9.35	Sitting on the table in home corner	Kate and Jessie	'Come on Ade, you can be the baby'	Said by Kate. Ade lay on the carpet
9.40	Riding bike	Kate and Jessie	'Kate, Kate!'	Ade calling excitedly
9.50	Outdoor sand	Kate	'Me have that'	Ade grabbing sand mould
9.55				
10.00				
10.05				
10.10				
10.15				

Date: __9.8.02__

Identification of child: __Ade__   Age: __4__

Researcher: __Meg Jones__

top. Tick against each child for the activity they are involved in (as in the completed outdoor 'Observation tick chart' on page 71).

➤ Use the tick chart to assess the skills of individual children. For example, 'Can hold a pencil correctly', 'Can use scissors', 'Can read three letter words' and 'Can stand on one foot'. Use ticks and crosses in the boxes.

Support and extension
Ensure that methods of observation recording are appropriate to the age and ability of the children.

Evaluation
Evaluate your findings after each observation. What can you conclude? Did the descriptive observation recording tell you something new about the child, or confirm what you already knew? Use observations for assessment.

Supporting activity
Use the results of your observations to plan future activities, highlight any additional support needed and identify any ongoing problems.

Case study
➤ **C16.1**: 4, 5, 6, 7, 8 ·   ·

Holly screams and runs to her key worker with teeth marks in her arm while Cory carries on playing, oblivious to the distress he has caused. This is the third time this week this has happened. You decide to observe Cory to see when and why he bites other children. How will you observe Cory and how will you use the results? Write down the case study with your responses for your portfolio.

Follow on
➤ **C16.1**: 2 · · · · · · ·

Always obtain written permission before observing children; if parents object you must not observe their child. You will need to inform parents that you will be making observations, potentially for the period of the award. If there are particular concerns, the most appropriate member of staff should discuss them with the parents. Follow the policies of the setting.

Questions
(See answer pointers at end of chapter.)

➤ **C16.1**: 5 · · · · · · ·   **1.** How can you minimise distractions during your observations?
➤ **C16.1**: 6 · · · · · · ·   **2.** How can you gain information from a child to assess their progress?
➤ **C16.1**: 4, 7 · · · · · ·   **3.** What role can an observer play to help children demonstrate their full potential?

Record the questions and your full answers and share with your assessor.

Did you know?

Some parents are concerned at the use of photographs of their children in portfolios. Always seek parental permission first.

C16.1: 2

Extra idea

➤ Use the 'Event sampling chart' photocopiable sheet on page 147 to record a child's movements every one, two, five or ten minutes over a set period of time. (See the completed 'Event sampling chart' opposite.) This will show behaviour such as interests, concentration, contact with peers, isolation and unacceptable behaviour. Evaluate your findings.

C16.1: 3   ◀

Element C16.2 Use observation results to inform the children's future care and education

It is not expected that your assessor will directly observe you for this Unit. The activity presented can be used as an opportunity to observe a child. If this happens then you will need a colleague to lead the activity while you concentrate on recording the interaction between child and child, between child and adult, and the skills used. If you do not observe at this time and your assessor directly observes you with the pattern-making activity, it will provide evidence for **C3**, **C10**, and **C11**. You can be questioned on the theoretical outcomes of any observations you make in the care and education of a particular child, or the group as a whole, as evidence of knowledge for **C16.2**.

Pattern making

Number of children: six.

Resources

Paint; plates or shallow trays; sugar paper; fruit, such as oranges, apples and star fruit; vegetables, such as carrots, potatoes and broccoli; bowl; knife; chopping board; table covering; aprons.

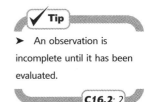

✔ Tip

➤ An observation is incomplete until it has been evaluated.

C16.2: 2

Preparation

Plan the activity using the 'Activity plan' photocopiable sheet on page 131. Ensure all the fruit and vegetables are clean and firm. Protect the table and let the children choose various coloured paints. Pour a thin layer of paint on to each plate or tray. Leave on one side with enough paper for each child.

What to do

➤ Place the fruit and vegetable bowl in the centre of the table and talk about the contents with the group. Identify each one as a fruit or vegetable, describe its shape and colour, ask the children if it has a smell and pass it round for the children to feel and smell.

➤ Continue the discussion as you slice each piece. Ask the children what they expect to find inside and whether it will be different to the outside.
➤ Cut the oranges, apples and star fruit in half around the middle to show the segments, the arrangements of pips and the amazing star shape.
➤ Cut the carrots across to provide circles, the potatoes in half and then cut shapes such as a triangle or square into the flat side, and finally the broccoli into florets and then again in half lengthways to provide a flat side.
➤ Give the children a piece of paper each and encourage them to dip the fruit or vegetable pieces in the paint and print patterns on the paper.
➤ Encourage the children to use the prints in an imaginative way, as repeating patterns or to tell a story, using an orange shape for the sun or the star shape for the night sky.

Support and extension
Use fewer shapes for younger children, and cut pieces that are easy to hold. Ensure the children do not attempt to eat the painted fruit and vegetables. Older children can have more and smaller pieces.

Evaluation
Were the children interested? Were the pieces too slippery? Can you think of other food that would make good printing blocks? How can you further develop the children's knowledge and understanding of fruit and vegetables?

Supporting activity
In this session, record group interaction, individual children's responses to the paint, fruit and vegetables, sensory experiences, language and creativity.

➤ *C16.2*: 1, 2, 3, 4, · · ·
5, 6, *cross-
reference to **C11**
and **C7***

Case study
Due to his poorly-developed language, four-year-old Alex has his fees paid by Social Services. The practitioners and children had previously found it difficult to understand him, so he became frustrated and started shouting and throwing things around. His mother was persuaded to take him for speech therapy. Within a very short time he began to make himself understood and the anti-social behaviour started diminishing. However, his mother has complained that he has started swearing. How will you plan an observation of Alex to establish what is happening in the setting? What possible actions can you expect to take as a result of your assessment? Write down the case study with your responses for your portfolio.

Follow on
Consider how you can approach an observation of a child for whom English is a second language. What sort of assistance might you require for this task? What, if any, difficulties might you encounter? Can cultural differences be significant? How can you evaluate the findings?

Questions
(See answer pointers at end of chapter.)

➤ *C16.2*: 4 · · · · · · · · **4.** *What do you need to be aware of in your responsibilities as an observer?* ◄

➤ **5.** *If you feel changes need to be made to the individual care of a child, or the*   ***C16.2***: 5   ◄
curriculum plan, who are the relevant individuals that you may need to consult?

➤ **6.** *Describe the observation and assessment techniques you can use to establish*   ***C16.2***: 1, 2, 6   ◄
patterns of behaviour. Indicate how to use these to develop curriculum plans.

Record the questions and your full answers and share with your assessor.

> ### Did you know?
> Job roles for people qualified with an NVQ Level 3 include Nursery supervisor, Pre-school leader, Crèche leader, Playgroup leader, Toy library leader, Special educational needs supporter, Nursery nurse, Nanny and Childminder. For more information visit: www.qca.org.uk

Extra idea
➤ Use a computer programme to record some of your findings. Alternate bar   ***C16.2***: 1, 2   ◄
charts, line graphs and pie charts with the same information to see which
gives a clearer presentation of the evidence.

Practical ways of collecting evidence
It is helpful to have a long-term study of an individual child to plot progress in
a number of developmental areas. In addition to this, several short
observations, on specific events and individual behaviour, will give you an
insight into possible uses of observation and assessment. Try several different
techniques and ways of recording and evaluate the usefulness of these.

> ### Check your progress
> It is unlikely that you will be assessed while observing children. However,
> you will be questioned on your observations and evaluations. You should
> also have witness testimonies from colleagues to confirm that you have
> carried out the observations in an appropriate manner. Other forms of
> evidence include reflective accounts of your performance, plans for
> preparing activities and the observation itself, and case studies.

Answer pointers
Ensure your answers are fully made for your assessor.
1. Other staff cover. Unobtrusive. Pick appropriate time. Staff aware.
2. Questioning. Prompting. Asking to perform actions. Suggestions.
3. Type of observation. Participant or non-participant. Confidence. Trust.
4. Non-judgemental. Objective. Do not interfere. Unbiased. Professional.
5. Senior colleagues. Parents. Teacher. SENCO. Other professionals.
6 Pre-coded categories. Planning. Structured description. Discussion. Free
description. Evaluation.

Further information
A Practical Guide to Child Observation and Assessment by Christine Hobart
and Jill Frankel (Nelson Thornes, 2001)

E3 Plan and equip environments for children

This Unit refers to aspects relating to the safety and suitability of the physical environment, including furniture, equipment and emergency procedures.

This chapter will enable you to:
E3.1 Establish and maintain a safe environment for children
E3.2 Establish and carry out safety and emergency procedures
E3.3 Select furniture and equipment for children
E3.4 Organise and maintain the physical environment for children.

Element E3.1 Establish and maintain a safe environment for children

➤ *E3.1: range 2b, 3a* · · Your assessor can observe and question you. ◄

Barfi
Number of children: six.

✓ Tip

➤ Confirm who is responsible for checking the first aid box, the frequency of checks, if checks are recorded and the list of contents.

E3.1: 7

➤ Ensure that you know where all records relating to safety checks and action taken are kept.

E3.1: 9, 10

Resources
200g condensed milk; 250g full cream milk powder; food colouring; icing sugar to roll out; crushed cardamom seeds and pistachio nuts or teaspoon of vanilla essence and silver balls; mixing bowl; spoons; rolling-pins; blunt knife; boards.

Preparation
Plan the activity using the 'Activity plan' photocopiable sheet on page 131. Ask for permission from parents and carers to taste foods and check for any food allergies or dietary requirements. Clean the tables and ask the children to wash their hands and put on aprons. Empty the milk into the mixing bowl.

What to do
➤ Ask the children to mix the milk powder into the condensed milk to make a stiff dry dough. Add food colouring and flavourings before it is fully mixed.
➤ Ask the children to wash their hands while the mixture hardens for 20 to 30 minutes.
➤ Dust the boards with icing sugar and roll the dough to 5mm thick. Help the children cut it into diamonds and decorate with nuts and silver balls.
➤ Encourage the children to wash the utensils and clean down the tables.

Support and extension
Assist the younger children. Encourage older children to make more shapes. ◄

➤ *Cross-reference to* · · ·
C10

Evaluation
Did the children wash their hands thoroughly? Did they need assistance? Did they enjoy the barfi? What other traditional foods can you make together?

Supporting activity
Encourage visitors from the community to come in at various times throughout the year to share their cultural experiences relating to food.

> **Case study**
> To ensure the children are aware of health and safety issues when keeping pets at the setting, what areas will you cover and how you will develop them? Write down the case study with your responses for your portfolio.
>
> **Follow on**
> Find out about the diseases that can be caught from animals, what the treatments are and whether there are any long-term consequences.

E3.1: 11 ◄

Questions
(See answer pointers at end of chapter.)
> **1.** *What are the statutory adult:child ratios and good practice for your setting?* **E3.1**: 1 ◄
> **2.** *What are the relevant regulations and appropriate practice for the use and* · · **E3.1**: 4, 6 ◄
> *storage of cleaning equipment, materials and potentially dangerous substances?*
> **3.** *What safety checks need to be made for an outdoor play area?* · · · · · · · · **E3.1**: 9 ◄

Record the questions and your full answers and share these with your assessor.

> **Did you know?**
> Chemist shops sell a plastic cylinder to check if equipment is suitable for young children. If an object slips inside the tube, a small child can choke on it.
>
>
>
> **E3.1**: 9

Extra idea
> Indicate safety factors and potential hazards to your assessor. You may be · · · **E3.1**: 2, 4, 5, 8, 12 ◄
> questioned on the environment and health and safety issues.

Element E3.2 Establish and carry out safety and emergency procedures

> Your assessor can observe and question you. · **E3.2**: range 1b ◄

Safety squares game
Number of children: two to four.

Resources
'Accident game' photocopiable sheet on page 148; A4 card; scissors; laminator.

Tip

➤ Check who the authorised first aid personnel are in your setting. Enrol yourself on a first aid course as soon as you can.

E3.2: 6

Preparation

Plan the activity using the 'Activity plan' photocopiable sheet on page 131. Make two card copies of the 'Accident game', cut out the boxes and laminate.

What to do

➤ Invite the children to pick a card and ask a related 'What if...?' question.
➤ Lead the questions down a projected path, such as, 'What if we make a 999 call, who will come?' and, 'If there is a fire what do we have to do?'.
➤ Reassure, but also reinforce the need to know what to do in an emergency.
➤ Use this opportunity to discuss any of the children's concerns.

Support and extension

Ask younger children to talk about the illustrations. Invite older children to read the captions. Encourage all the children to join in the conversation.

Evaluation

Did the children need more preparation? Can you play this game with just one child who is fearful of accidents and emergencies? Write up your experiences and evaluation of this activity for your portfolio.

Supporting activity

In June, every year, it is National Child Safety Week, sponsored by the Child Accident Prevention Trust (www.capt.org.uk). Information and resources are also available from the Royal Society for the Prevention of Accidents (www.rospa.org.uk) and your local Environmental Health Department.

➤ *E3.2: 7* · · · · · · · ·
Case study
You have been asked to review the setting's fire drill procedure. Where will you start? What documentation will you read? Who will you talk to? Outline the process and suggest any changes you may recommend for consideration. Write down the case study with your responses for your portfolio.

➤ *E3.2: 8* · · · · · · · ·
Follow on
Consider the difference between a fire evacuation and a bomb scare evacuation. Find out how they need to be treated differently and why.

Questions
(See answer pointers at end of chapter.)

➤ *E3.2: 2, 4* · · · · · · · · **4.** *What information do you require from parents for use in case of emergency? Where and how should this be kept?*

➤ *E3.2: 7, 8* · · · · · · · · **5.** *When, how and why are emergency procedures rehearsed?*

➤ *E3.2: 10* · · · · · · · · **6.** *What are the reporting procedures for accidents or incidents in the setting?*
Record the questions and your full answers and share these with your assessor.

Did you know?

Accident figures show most baby injuries occur with baby walkers. This is due to children falling into furniture or down stairs, burning themselves, falling on fires, and scalds or poisoning as they grasp items normally out of reach.

E3.2: 2

Extra idea

➤ Draw up a safety plan for an imaginary setting. Consider who should be · · · · **E3.2**: 2 ◄
consulted and what should be included. Discuss with your assessor.

Element E3.3 Select furniture and equipment for children

➤ Your assessor can observe and question you. · · · · · · · · · · · · · · · **E3.3**: range 1a ◄

Little and large

Number of children: four.

Resources

Tape measure; paper; pencils; scissors; clipboards; equipment catalogues; glue.

Preparation

Plan the activity using the 'Activity plan' photocopiable sheet on page 131.

What to do

➤ Explain to the children that we can judge how big something is by measuring it. Point out the numbers along the length of the measure.

➤ Let the children choose pictures of furniture similar to that in the setting.

➤ Help the children cut out their pictures and glue them to the paper.

➤ Clip the pages to the clipboards and help them measure the real furniture.

✔ **Tip**

➤ Find out how and when furniture is checked, cleaned and maintained in your setting, in order to maintain a safe and healthy environment.

E3.3: 3

Support and extension

➤ Keep the explanations simple for younger children. Encourage older children to recognise and write the numbers they can see on the tape measure.

Cross-reference to ◄
C10, **C25**

Evaluation

Did the children understand the activity? What other ways of measuring will have meaning to the children, such as building blocks and paper size?

Supporting activity

➤ Make your own selection of furniture. Indicate age specifications, furniture · · · **E3.2**: 1, 3, 5, 6 ◄
combinations, storage combinations, safety features and the basis for your choice.

➤ **E3.3**: 1, 2 · · · · · · · ·

Case study
You are responsible for selecting the furniture and equipment for a new pre-school room. Draw a room plan, indicating the furniture position and where the different activities take place. Indicate why you have made your choices. Write down the case study with your responses for your portfolio. ◄

Follow on

➤ **E3.3**: 2 · · · · · · · ·   Identify four activities or pieces of equipment to develop the learning opportunities, for the six Areas of Learning, for three- to five-year-olds. ◄

Questions
(See answer pointers at end of chapter.)

➤ **E3.3**: 1, 3 · · · · · · · · **7.** *What must you consider so fixtures and furniture are safe for the setting?* ◄
➤ **E3.3**: 4 · · · · · · · · **8.** *How can careful selection of furniture and soft furnishings reflect the cultures* ◄ *of the children in the setting and create a homely environment?*
➤ **E3.3**: 5 · · · · · · · · **9.** *Describe different types of storage equipment and why they are appropriate.* ◄

Record the questions and your full answers and share these with your assessor.

Did you know?
Visit the British Standards Institute's website to find out about safety tests on equipment designed for use with children: www.bsi-global.com/education

Extra idea

➤ **E3.3**: 3 · · · · · · · ·   Investigate the symbols on equipment and furniture that indicate its suitability ◄ for use with young children. Include the Kitemark, the Lion symbol, and the CE sign. Consult your local Trading Standards office.

Element E3.4 Organise and maintain the physical environment for children

➤ **E3.4**: range 1a · · · ·   Your assessor can observe and question you. ◄

Follow-my-leader
Number of children: four.

Resources
Four clipboards; paper; pencils; nature books; books showing buildings and outdoor features similar to ones seen in the immediate environment.

Preparation
Plan the activity using the 'Activity plan' photocopiable sheet on page 131. Draw a map of a suitable area to take the children, with a cross and number at the areas you propose to stop. Copy the map for the children.

What to do

➤ Tell the children that they are going to play 'Follow-my-leader' around the outside play area.

➤ Ensure that the children are suitably clothed for the weather.

➤ Give each child a map and point out the route and stopping places.

➤ As you stop at each point, discuss what you can see, hear, touch and smell. Invite the children to note the features, landscape and living things.

➤ At stopping points, ask the children to note the number on their paper and write or draw something of interest that they can see.

➤ Talk about health and safety issues, such as not climbing on walls.

➤ Discuss the findings. Use books to reinforce and learn new facts and words.

> ✓ **Tip**
> ➤ Draw up a checklist for maintenance procedures in your setting.
>
> **E3.4**: 1

Support and extension

➤ Restrict the tour to two or three stops for younger children. Invite older · · · · children to explore the area in greater detail and draw their own maps.

Cross-reference to ◄
C10, C24

Evaluation

Did you have too many or too few stopping points? Did you develop unplanned experiences? How can you develop this idea for a theme?

Supporting activity

➤ Encourage the children to paint, draw and write health and safety posters, · · · such as, 'Put litter in the bin', 'Take care of our plants' and 'Close the gate'. Laminate the posters and display in appropriate places.

Cross-reference to ◄
C24

Case study

➤ Jenny is starting soon at your setting and has mobility difficulties. She wears a leg splint and uses a walking aid. When reviewing your environment to see if any adaptations need to be made, what things will you need to consider? Write down the case study with your responses for your portfolio.

E3.4: 6 ◄

Follow on

➤ Consider other disabilities and impairments and what adaptations you will need to make for children with special needs. How many of these changes can you implement as part of a regular review of the furniture and equipment layout and planned improvements?

Cross-reference to ◄
C17

Questions

(See answer pointers at end of chapter.)

➤ **10.** *What should be considered to ensure the best use of space for activities* · · · **E3.4**: 2 ◄
and free movement of all in the setting?

➤ **11.** *How can you guarantee that standards of cleanliness ensure the health* · · · **E3.4**: 3 ◄
and safety of everyone in the setting?

➤ **12.** *In what ways can you improve the physical environment of a setting, at* · · · **E3.4**: 6 ◄
minimal expense, to accommodate children with visual impairment?

Record the questions and your full answers and share these with your assessor.

Did you know?

Many of the common plants are highly poisonous, causing allergies or irritation. Supervise children and wash hands after touching natural materials.

E3.4: 7

Extra idea

➤ **E3.4**: 7 · · · · · · · · Use the 'Design a play area' photocopiable sheet on page 149 to cut and paste your own design of a safe play area. Share the finished product with your assessor, explaining your safety concerns and reasoning. ◄

Practical ways of collecting evidence

The need for a healthy and safe environment is pertinent to every aspect of childcare. Over a period of one month, collect newspaper clippings about children involved in accidents. Assess the different kinds of incidents and suggest ways of protecting the children in your care. Discuss with your assessor, who can question you, and record your findings in your portfolio.

Check your progress

With careful planning, you can cover much of this Unit by direct observation. You are expected to be observed covering at least one of each of the range statements for all four Elements. Witness testimonies, reflective accounts, work products and assignments can cover the performance criteria not seen.

Answer pointers

Ensure your answers are fully made for your assessor.

1. 1:3. 1:4. 1:8. Minimum of two staff. Maximum of 26 children per group.
2. COSHH. Lock. Use correctly. Not decant in different containers. Supervise.
3. Fences intact. Gates fastened. Glass. Water. Safe equipment. Supervision.
4. Name(s). Responsible adults. Telephone. Confidentially. Accurate.
5. Respond quickly. Regularly. Practice. Ensure safety. Review. Prevention.
6. Policy. Prompt. Accurate. All details. Parents informed.
7. Height. Size. Stability. Accessibility. Finish. Mobility. Safety symbols.
8. Cushions. Curtains. Sofa. Patterns. Colours. Fabrics.
9. Size. Access. Locked or open. Trays. Variety. Shelves. Cupboards. Boxes.
10. Positioning of fixtures. Furniture. Access. Dimension. Rotation.
11. Monitor. Policies. Dedicated staff. Equipment. Clean materials. Training.
12. Coloured strips. Directional footprints. Fixed positions. Large print.

Further information

Safety for Home-based Child Care by Rosie Mercer (Child Accident Prevention Trust, 2001)

How Big Is It? by Meg Jones (Ginn, 2001)

M7 Plan, implement and evaluate learning activities and experiences

This Unit includes long-, medium- and short-term plans for activities and experiences in all the major curriculum areas. Plans are used to promote physical, social and emotional, sensory and intellectual, and language and communication development. Also included are individual learning plans.

This chapter will enable you to:

M7.1 Plan a curriculum to facilitate children's learning and development
M7.2 Develop Individual Learning Programmes for children
M7.3 Implement planned learning activities and experiences
M7.4 Evaluate planned learning activities and experiences.

Element M7.1 Plan a curriculum to facilitate children's learning and development

➤ Your assessor can question you. · **M7.1**: *range 1a, 3a, b* ◄

Patterns in the curriculum

Pattern opportunities occur throughout the routine and within the curriculum areas every day. Ideas for short-term planning are focused on here.
Number of children: six.

Resources

Resources appropriate to the activity.

Preparation

You will need to be able to prepare curriculum plans. Use the 'Long-term planning' photocopiable sheet on page 150. On a monthly basis, identify your main themes and the subject areas under the Areas of Learning. On the 'Medium-term planning' photocopiable sheet, on page 151, detail what you intend covering over three months. Use the 'Short-term planning' photocopiable sheet on page 152 to plan your daily activities. Use the 'Activity plan' photocopiable sheet, on page 131, for individual activities to pinpoint what you are trying to achieve. Preparation as appropriate to activities.

What to do

➤ **Personal and social development** – Visit places of worship with the children and look at patterns, such as tiles and symbols. Encourage children

Tip

➤ Where activities have been planned for other Units they should be cross-referenced into **M7**.

to spot patterns around them.

➤ **Communication, language and literacy** – Play word games with missing and rhyming words. Use patterns of orientation, such as left to right and top to bottom. Reinforce the beginning, middle and end of a story.

➤ **Mathematical development** – Show the children how to make symmetrical patterns using squared paper. Devise number pattern sequences with missing numbers to guess. Look at door numbers. Clap in a regular pattern.

➤ **Knowledge and understanding of the world** – Discuss patterns on butterflies and petals. Compare shape, size and colour of birds. Develop a project on weather patterns and seasons. Design patterns for a plate.

➤ **Physical development** – Encourage the children to make their bodies form patterns. Develop a movement sequence of hopping, running and jumping.

➤ **Creative development** – Print patterns using a variety of implements to create geometric shapes. Design mendhi patterns for hand decoration and rangoli patterns to put at the door of the home corner.

Support and extension

Choose activities appropriate to the abilities of the children. Some will need more help than others. Adapt the activities to suit individual children.

Evaluation

Did the children have any difficulty? Did the patterns provide an interesting way to introduce curriculum learning? Did you include multicultural aspects?

Supporting activity

Keep a 'Pattern book', with all your ideas for consultation when planning in the future, and try out some of them.

➤ **M7.1**: 5

Case study

Involve the whole team when planning. Your role is to ensure anti-discrimination and equal opportunities are considered when suggesting activities. What will you ask the team? What activities and learning experiences will you include? Write down the case study with your responses for your portfolio.

➤ Cross-reference to **C16**

Follow on

Do several short observations in various group-play situations to illustrate positive examples of equal opportunities. If you observe any negative actions, note these and follow with an evaluation of how to turn them into positive examples. Consider gender, ethnicity, disability and culture.

Questions

(See answer pointers at end of chapter.)

➤ **M7.1**: 3   **1.** *What criteria are used to develop overall curriculum plans?*

➤ **M7.1**: 6   **2.** *Identify community resources that can be included in your planning process.*

➤ **M7.1**: 7   **3.** *Why is it necessary to have a flexible approach to curriculum planning?*

Record the questions and your full answers and share these with your assessor.

Did you know?
Piaget, an eminent psychologist, made a special study of children's learning. He was convinced that the only way we gain knowledge is through a continual reconstructing of reality. He believed that we can never say, 'I have arrived', as there is always something ahead to learn. Curriculum plans enable us to provide opportunities for that continual learning process.

M7.1: 3

Extra idea
➤ Choose a theme to cover the six Areas of Learning. Copy the 'Spider chart' · · **M7.1**: 3 ◀
photocopiable sheet on page 132. Write the theme in the centre. In the surrounding boxes suggest two activities for each Area of Learning. In the last two spaces indicate the time scales and equal opportunities aspects.

Element M7.2 Develop Individual Learning Programmes for children

➤ Your assessor can question you. · **M7.2**: range 1b ◀

Counting to ten
Number of children: one-to-one or as part of a small group.

Resources
Resources appropriate to the activity.

Preparation
Plan the activity using the 'Activity plan' photocopiable sheet on page 131.

What to do
➤ Prepare a box of ten items of various types, such as cars, shells and beads. Include playing cards numbered 1 to 10. Provide a sorting tray. Ask a child to take a card and put the same number of one type of item on the tray.
➤ Use Asian sweets to count up to ten with.
➤ Encourage the children to count the number of times you clap.
➤ Put stickers on your fingers as characters to tell a story and to count.
➤ Count in different languages.
➤ Draw an outline of a purse and give the children ten coins. Ask them to place a specified number of coins in the purse.

Support and extension
Use numbers children are confident with. Increase until the target is met.

Evaluation
Are some activities more appealing to certain children than others? Can you make a game for everyone to join in? Record the results to monitor progress.

✓ **Tip**
➤ Ensure recordings are made regularly, according to the requirements of the programme, to assess their progress.

M7.2: 4

➤ **M7.2**: *1, 2* · · · · · · ·

Supporting activity

Keep statements on Individual Learning Programmes simple and achievable, such as, 'To put reading book in correct drawer at school' and, 'To hang up and collect coat without being reminded'. ◄

➤ **M7.2**: *1, 2, 4, 5* · · · ·

Case study

Bethany is six and finds co-ordination slighty difficult. You want to target hand–eye co-ordination. Complete an Individual Learning Programme for her, identifying the action you will take and an outline of activities to meet her target. Write down the case study with your responses for your portfolio. ◄

➤ *Cross-reference to* · · ·
C3

Follow on

Find out what is an appropriate level of development for a six-year-old. Compare the different abilities of children of the same age in your setting. They will all be slightly different. The aim of an Individual Learning Programme is to help a child slightly below the norm to catch up if possible. ◄

Questions

(See answer pointers at end of chapter.)

➤ **M7.2**: *1, 2, 3, 4, 5* · · **4.** *What are the key points when preparing an Individual Learning Programme?* ◄
➤ **M7.2**: *3, 5, 7* · · · · · **5.** *In what circumstances would you modify an Individual Learning Programme?* ◄
➤ **M7.2**: *3, 6* · · · · · · · **6.** *With whom would you discuss preparing an Individual Learning Programme?* ◄

Record the questions and your full answers and share these with your assessor.

Did you know?

'An infant coming into the world has no past, no experience in handling himself, no scale on which to judge his own worth. He must rely on the experiences he has with the people around him and the messages they give him about his worth as a person.'
V. Satir

➤ **M7.2**: *1, 3* · · · · · ·

Extra idea

If you have concerns about a child, draw up an Initial Concern Form to identify strengths, concerns, parental comments, action and who is involved. Follow this with an Individual Learning Programme specifying short-term targets, approaches, support and involvement. Review these at regular intervals. Ensure the child is an active participant in this process. ◄

Element M7.3 Implement planned learning activities and experiences

➤ Your assessor can observe and question you. · · · · · · · · · · · · · · · · *M7.3*: range *1a, 2a* ◄

Multicultural ideas

Many planned activities can be included in this Element. The following are some additional ideas that can be integrated into long-term plans.
Number of children: small or whole groups.

Resources

Resources appropriate to the activity.

Preparation

Plan the activity using the 'Activity plan' photocopiable sheet on page 131.

What to do

➤ Learn traditional songs and stories from a variety of cultures.
➤ Invite parents to a Divali party with Indian sweets, dancing and saris.
➤ Use African print fabrics to stimulate printing designs.
➤ Decorate the shells of hard-boiled eggs at Easter.
➤ Decorate red envelopes with gold pens for Chinese New Year.
➤ Make kites to use on a windy day.

> ✓ **Tip**
>
> ➤ Plans from your setting that you have not worked on personally are not evidence for your NVQ. All evidence must be your own work.

Support and extension

Keep the activity simple for younger children. Older children will be able to elaborate or decorate, as appropriate.

Evaluation

Individual activities may be planned as part of a wider topic. You may wish to have a traditional story or song, decorate plates and act out a play, covering many areas of development.

Supporting activity

➤ Devise a theme incorporating different activities over a period of time. Cover all aspects of the curriculum including diversity. Record your long-term, medium-term and short-term plans for inclusion in your portfolio.

M7.3: 1 ◄

Case study

➤ You have been asked to lead the pre-school group. The previous leader kept control of all activities, placing them in areas around the room, and replacing with another set at a particular time. How will you be more flexible? Write down the case study with your responses for your portfolio.

M7.3: 4 ◄

Follow on

➤ Consider the layout of the setting and how conducive it is to delivering a full curriculum. Supposing you are in a position to order new resources, equipment and furniture, what will you choose?

M7.3: 3 ◄

Questions

(See answer pointers at end of chapter.)

➤ **M7.3**: 2 · · · · · · · · **7.** *How can you ensure health and safety requirements are met within the* ◄
curriculum plans and Individual Learning Programmes?

➤ **M7.3**: 5 · · · · · · · · **8.** *How can you ensure individual needs are met and interest sustained?* ◄

➤ **M7.3**: 7 · · · · · · · · **9.** *How can you plan for spontaneous and unplanned learning opportunities?* ◄

Record the questions and your full answers and share these with your assessor.

> ### Did you know?
>
> In her book, *The Early Years: Laying the Foundations for Racial Equality* (Trentham Books, 1994), Iram Siraj-Blatchford uses the heading 'High Quality Provision Requires High Quality Training'. To provide the best care, to understand and value the curriculum and offer to inclusive provision, we need to always be learning.

Extra idea

➤ **M7.3**: range 1b, · · · · Use the 'Long-term planning', 'Medium-term planning' and 'Short-term ◄
2a, b, c   planning' photocopiable sheets on pages 150, 151 and 152, to devise sample plans.

Element M7.4 Evaluate planned learning activities and experiences

➤ **M7.4**: range 2d · · · · Your assessor can question you. ◄

Evaluation of cutting and sticking

Number of children: six.

Resources

Resources appropriate to the activity.

Preparation

Plan the activity using the 'Activity plan' photocopiable sheet on page 131.

What to do

➤ Engage the children in cutting and sticking activities.
➤ Is glue suitable for use with young children and is it used correctly?
➤ Do the children have the necessary physical skills?
➤ Can children with disabilities and impairments participate in this activity?
➤ Are left- and right-handed scissors available?
➤ Have plastic or less sharp, round-ended scissors been provided?
➤ Are scissors with decorative cutter blades available for older children?
➤ Are bright colours provided for children with a visual impairment?
➤ Is the end product valued more than the process?
➤ Did any children progress their skills further than previously managed?
➤ Have the children been encouraged and praised?

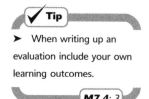

✔ **Tip**

➤ When writing up an evaluation include your own learning outcomes.

M7.4: 3

Support and extension

Support younger children by providing extra help with cutting and gluing large objects. Encourage older children to make finer more elaborate products.

Evaluation

The evaluation of an activity should be made by asking many pertinent questions. Evaluation is not an end in itself, it should be used for future planning to meet the children's needs.

Supporting activity

Evaluate another activity, such as story-telling or sand-play.

Case study

➤ Every afternoon Wilfred's mother expects a completed piece of work to take home with him. As he is anxious, a member of staff helps him make something 'recognisable'. Wilfred no longer tries to make anything himself. How can an evaluation help him with his development? How will you use the information? Write down the case study with your responses for your portfolio.

M7.4: 1, 7, 8 ◄

Follow on

➤ Design a series of posters, to be placed round the room, for each of the major curriculum areas, to help inexperienced staff. Indicate the learning that children gain from the activity. Share your rough copies with your assessor.

M7.4: 2 ◄

Questions

(See answer pointers at end of chapter.)

➤ **10.** *What should you be aware of, if evaluating an activity you are part of?* · · · **M7.4**: 3 ◄

➤ **11.** *Why is it thought children learn more from spontaneous learning?* · · · · · **M7.4**: 4 ◄

➤ **12.** *How can children become actively involved in the evaluation process?* · · · · **M7.4**: 6, 7 ◄

Record the questions and your full answers and share these with your assessor.

Did you know?

'Good planning is the key to making children's learning effective, exciting, varied and progressive. Good planning enables practitioners to build up knowledge about how individual children learn and make progress. It also provides opportunities for practitioners to think and talk about how to sustain a successful learning environment.' *Planning for Learning in the Foundation Stage* (QCA, 2001).

Extra idea

➤ **M7.4**: 5 · · · · · · · · · Have a safety audit of activities available to children on a specific day. Evaluate ◄ your findings. Was everything being carried out in a safe manner? Were there any dangers? Discuss your findings with your assessor.

Practical ways of collecting evidence

You may evaluate the activities in different ways. You may record an activity as a reflective account after the event, or you may keep an ongoing tick chart. If you are observing individuals you can cross-reference this into **C16**.

Check your progress

Your assessor will not directly observe you planning, developing or evaluating the learning programmes, but the implementation of those processes. This will occur on many occasions and will be covered in other Units. Ensure all relevant documentation is cross-referenced into this Unit. You will need to be able to draw up plans. Other evidence may come from reflective accounts, witness testimonies, photographs, child observations linked to learning programmes and log books showing unplanned activities.

Answer pointers

Ensure your answers are fully made for your assessor.
1. Appropriate. Areas of Learning. Early Learning Goals. Variety. Challenging.
2. Shops. School-crossing patroller. Fire station and fire fighters. Community police officer. School nurse. Faith buildings and faith leaders.
3. Unplanned. Choice. Spontaneous. Weather. Staff changes. Interest.
4. Realistic. Uncomplicated. Attainable. Appropriate. Fit curriculum plan. After discussion. Specific. Recorded. Safe.
5. After consideration. Under health and safety. Parents. Achievement. Change. Spontaneous opportunities.
6. Parents. Colleagues. SENCO. Child. Confidentiality. Key worker. Specialist.
7. Correct use. Manufacturers instructions. Safety policy.
8. Within attention span. Ability to choose. Achievable. Interesting.
9. Aware of personal events. Plan for appropriate times. Listen.
10. Objective. How directive. Extend language. Interact. Influence. Encourage.
11. Grab interest. Use of resources. Share. Immediate. Play not 'work'.
12. Interact. Question. Observe. Share. Discussion. Parental feedback.

Further information

Planning Play and the Early Years by Penny Tassoni and Karen Hucker (Heinemann Education, 2000)
Special Needs Handbook by Dr Hannah Mortimer (Scholastic, 2002)
Planning for Learning in the Foundation Stage (QCA, 2001)
Foundation Themes series (Scholastic, 2003)
Goals for the Foundation Stage series (Scholastic, 2003)

P2 Establish and maintain relationships with parents

This Unit includes developing ongoing relationships with parents, when children are settling in, exchanging information about health and welfare, how the children are getting on and sharing the care and management.

This chapter will enable you to:

P2.1 Develop relationships with parents new to the setting
P2.2 Plan settling-in arrangements with parents
P2.3 Exchange information with parents about their children
P2.4 Share the care and management of children with their parents.

Element P2.1 Develop relationships with parents new to the setting

➤ Your assessor can question you. · *P2.1: range 1a, b* ◄

Home-link activity
Number of children: one-to-one.

Resources
Card binder, cardboard wallet, plastic pocket or plastic packet, as relevant, for each child; resources appropriate to the activity.

Preparation
Arrange a visit to the setting or home. Prepare the home-link package.

What to do
➤ Prepare a welcome booklet. Include timings, lunch arrangements, PE requirements, the names of the staff. Translate if appropriate.
➤ Include practical activities to do at home. Examples are given below:

♦ A worksheet asking the child to write in their name and draw a picture of their family. Show the parent the preferred script to use.

♦ Numbered squares to glue pictures on, to develop fine motor skills.

♦ A selection of simple games using everyday objects in the home.

Tip

➤ Early on in your contact establish the preferred names of both children and parents. Use the correct names, even if difficult to pronounce, rather than giving an Anglicised nickname, as this is unacceptable to many people.

P2.1: 2

Support and extension

Ensure the activities are appropriate to the age and stage of the child.

Evaluation

Ask parents for feedback and adjust accordingly. Was the home-link package beneficial? Did you think through its effect on a parent and child starting in the setting?

Supporting activity

Share any correspondence to parents for your home-link package with your assessor, explaining your reasons for the specific content.

➤ **P2.1**: 3 · · · · · · · ·

Case study
Chloe, whose mother is deaf, will be starting in your setting soon. How can you prepare yourself and the setting, to meet both people's needs? Write down the case study with your responses for your portfolio. ◄

➤ **P2.1**: 9 · · · · · · · ·

Follow on
In a diverse community, what actions can be taken to ensure parents feel they can contribute to the effectiveness of the setting? Where can you get help from? Are there resources in the community you can call on? ◄

Questions
(See answer pointers at end of chapter.)

➤ **P2.1**: 1 · · · · · · · · **1.** *In what ways can you make parents feel positively welcomed into the setting?* ◄
➤ **P2.1**: 5, 8 · · · · · · · **2.** *When parents discuss their child, what are the important points to remember?* ◄
➤ **P2.1**: 6, 7 · · · · · · **3.** *What should be considered when giving parents information about the setting?* ◄

Record the questions and your full answers and share these with your assessor.

Did you know?
'Parent' comes from the Latin '*parere*', meaning 'to develop' or 'to bring forth'.

Extra idea
Some activities, such as cooking, require a lot of help or supervision. Parents can provide extra pairs of hands as well as cookery skills.

Element P2.2 Plan settling-in arrangements with parents

➤ **P2.2**: range 1a, e · · Your assessor can observe and question you. ◄

Parents at play
Number of children: available for all children.

Resources
A full range of curricular and extra-curricular equipment, toys and materials.

Preparation
Prepare a series of topic web sheets using the 'Topic web' photocopiable sheet on page 153. Invite parents to an open evening without the children.

What to do
➤ Set out the playroom with the regular range of activities.
➤ Place a topic web sheet by each activity showing the learning experiences.
➤ Ensure enough staff are available to discuss the learning opportunities.
➤ Discuss settling-in arrangements in this relaxed informal atmosphere.

✔ Tip

➤ Parents frequently have little time to spend settling a child into a setting. Try to encourage them to arrange to go in to work a little later on the first few mornings. Everyone will feel better if the child is left happy and playing rather than distressed.

Support and extension
Talk to the parents as they may have concerns. Reassure them and show them alternative activities if available.

Evaluation
Were there areas that can be improved upon? Did the topic webs stimulate discussion and give information? Did they help you when preparing them?

Supporting activity
Every setting receiving Education Grant Funding will have a copy of the QCA document, *Curriculum Guidance for the Foundation Stage*. Familiarise yourself with this as it contains a wealth of information on children's learning.

➤ **P2.2**: 3, 8 · · · · · · ·

Case study

Kruz is three and has had a childminder since he was six months old. He attends a childcare group, where he has made a number of friends. However, as the only black child, his mother is anxious in case he does not settle in the new setting. How would you advise and reassure Kruz's mother? Write down the case study with your responses for your portfolio. ◀

Follow on

Consider cultural differences in family life and childcare that impact on a child.

Questions

(See answer pointers at end of chapter.)

➤ **P2.2**: 3 · · · · · · · · · **4.** *When making arrangements with the parent about the settling-in period,* ◀
what factors do you need to take account of?

➤ **P2.2**: 4, 5 · · · · · · · **5.** *What information should you give a parent about collecting a child, and why?* ◀

➤ **P2.2**: 6, 7 · · · · · · · **6.** *If anxious about a child settling in, what reassurances can you give the parent?* ◀

Record the questions and your full answers and share these with your assessor.

Did you know?

Separation anxiety is the term used when a child is separated from the parents or main caregiver. Frequently the child cries and is clingy. Parents are also anxious at this time, but for different reasons.

C3.1: 5

Extra idea

➤ **P2.2**: 1 · · · · · · · · Write a list of all the information you would need to gain from a parent ◀
bringing a child to the setting for the first time.

Element P2.3 Exchange information with parents about their children

➤ **P2.3**: *range 1a, c,* · · · Your assessor can observe and question you. ◀
2a

Pre-school portfolio

Number of children: some small group work and one-to-one.

Resources

Folder with plastic pockets for each child; large label.

✔ **Tip**

➤ Talk to parents about not setting unrealistic goals and targets for their children.

Preparation

As appropriate to the chosen activity.

What to do

➤ Invite the children to write their name on the label, decorate it and stick it

to the front of their folder.
➤ Over time select A4-size or smaller pieces of the children's work to include.
➤ Let the children select photos from outings they have been involved in.
➤ Add a completed 'Development chart' photocopiable sheet from page 142.
➤ Keep in an accessible place for the children to retrieve, look at or add to.

Support and extension

Help younger children to write their name labels. Invite older children to choose the contents of their portfolio.

Evaluation

Were the children pleased with their portfolio? What other items can be included? What was the feedback from parents? Did it raise any issues?

Supporting activity

➤ Invite the parents to make a similar portfolio at home. . . . . *Cross-reference to* ◄
C11

Case study

➤ Daisy's mother is concerned her daughter is too lively in the evening. She *P2.3*: *3, 4, 6* ◄
will not go to bed at seven o'clock. Daisy falls asleep at 4pm at nursery.
How will you explain the setting's routine and the needs of the child to
her mother? Write down the case study with your responses for your
portfolio.

➤ ◄

Follow on

Discuss with your colleagues strategies for dealing with issues relating to *P2.3*: *3, 4, 5, 6*
differences in expectations between parents and the setting. Assess how
information is exchanged with parents and potential users in your setting.

Questions

(See answer pointers at end of chapter.)
➤ **7.** *What information do you need from parents and where should it be stored?* *P2.3*: *1* ◄
➤ **8.** *What information, in an ongoing process, do you need to have to enable* · · · *P2.3*: *2* ◄
you to better support and care for the child?
➤ **9.** *In what ways can you encourage parents to praise children's work?* · · · · · · *P2.3*: *7, 8* ◄

Record the questions and your full answers and share these with your assessor.

Did you know?
Try visiting: www.parentalk.co.uk, www.parentline.org.uk,
www.dfes.gov.uk/parents and www.childcarelink.gov.uk

Extra idea

➤ Take a sequence of photos showing child-centred learning, such as listening · · *P2.3*: *7, 8, cross-* ◄
to music, devising a dance, selecting costumes and performing the dance. *reference to* **C25**
Display the photos on a wall in sequence and invite the parents to see it.

Element P2.4 Share the care and management of children with their parents

➤ **P2.4**: range 1a, b, c · · Your assessor can observe and question you. ◀

Action planning

Number of children: all children and parents.

✓ Tip

➤ Adopt positive attitudes to parenting. Do not stereotype the male and female roles.

Resources

Blank book; coloured tabs; pen.

Preparation

Ask parents if they would like to help. Label the book 'Parent Helpers Action Book' and add the coloured tabs to a number of pages after the first three.

What to do

➤ Have a brain-storming session to identify the ways parents can help.
➤ In the book list the tasks, activities and skills that can be carried out.
➤ Provide some instruction where necessary on a tabbed page. Record the date the task is carried out. Record relevant information, such as where items are stored, how often the task needs doing and when. If everyone is busy, a parent can take the book and identify a task that has not been done already.
➤ Helpful areas include: storytelling; preparing and washing out paint pots; cooking; listening to readers; administrative work; talking to the children in their home language; library monitoring.
➤ The parent benefits by knowing they are welcome. The child is proud of their parent. The praticioner is relieved of some of the duties that can be shared. The parent sees routines in action and can question, comment and learn from them.

Support and extension

If a child finds it distressing to have a parent in the room, suggest the parent helps in another room or by taking things home to make and mend. If children are unable to cope with sharing their parent, it may be wise to wait a while, until they are emotionally secure enough to deal with the situation.

Evaluation

Are you comfortable working with parents? Were all parents able to contribute? Did issues arise that you had not planned for? If so, did you deal with these satisfactorily or do you need to seek further advice or training? What were the positive aspects coming out of the experience?

Supporting activity

Remember that not all parents will be able to read and write. Consider this when you offer them the 'Parent Helper Action Book'. Ask them if they are happy to use the book or would they prefer someone to identify the tasks required. This may give opportunities to lead parents into adult literacy classes.

➤ ### Case study
Sean's mother was burned as a child. She is anxious to know every detail of the emergency procedures. Sean is timid and easily distressed. How can you reassure Sean and his mother that in an emergency all necessary actions will be taken? Write down the case study with your responses for your portfolio.

P2.4: 2, 3   ◄

➤ ### Follow on
Consider how much knowledge you have to speak confidently to parents about behaviour problems, disorders, concerns or anxieties. Check out who the appropriate sources of advice are on different issues.

P2.3: 3, 4, 5   ◄

Questions
(See answer pointers at end of chapter.)
➤ **10.** *What should you consider, relating to the care of children and parents' wishes?* ·· *P2.4*: 1   ◄
➤ **11.** *Where can a parent seek advice about aspects of their children's care?* · · · *P2.4*: 4   ◄
➤ **12.** *Suggest strategies that you could use with parents, to manage children's* · · *P2.4*: 6   ◄
behaviour.

Record the questions and your full answers and share these with your assessor.

Did you know?
Research shows that interaction between the mother and child varies around the world. In Uganda, parents smile and coax a response from their child. In America parents stimulate their child. In Japan parents sooth their babies.

P2.4: 1

Extra ideas
➤ Use an imaginary situation to complete the photocopiable 'Parental action · · *P2.4*: 6   ◄
plan' sheet on page 154. Show how you would deal with the situation.

➤ Invite parents into the setting to observe their child. Provide a simple · · · · · *P2.4*: 5   ◄
observation sheet with questions asking what the child did, how, with whom, what happened, and what did they learn?

Practical ways of collecting evidence

Record all contact with parents, including dates and responses. These may be direct contact, telephone calls, at meetings, by letter or newsletter. Confirm this by asking a colleague, or a parent, for a witness testimony.

Check your progress

For some candidates, particularly those working in schools, collecting direct observations for this Unit can be difficult. Take whatever opportunities present themselves, as you need to be observed for one of the range statements in each of the four Elements. Other types of performance evidence can be collected through work products, reflective accounts, transferable skills from other Units, simulations and witness testimonies.

Answer pointers

Ensure your answers are fully made for your assessor.

1. Smile. Welcome. Involve. Coffee morning. Visit. Introduce. Ask advice.

2. They are experts. Listen. Confidential. Believe. Cultural variations. Respect.

3. Accurate. Reliable. Seek advice. Refer on. Consistent. Give confidence.

4. Child's needs. Parent's needs. Previous experience. Culture. Social factors.

5. Time. Person collecting. Signed agreement. Safety and security. Locking door or gate. Security passes or key pad numbers. Not letting others in.

6. Stay. Collect early. Telephone. Video link. Call in. Comforter.

7. Personal details. Medical history. Contact details. Preferences. Language. Special words. Comforters. Securely. Confidentially. Accessibly.

8. Change circumstances. New baby. Death in family. Move house. Illness.

9. Ask in. Personal portfolio. Take items home. Praise. Sharing achievements.

10. Family values. Expressed wishes. Policies. Practices. Procedures.

11. Senior colleague. Health Visitor. SENCO. School Nurse. General Practitioner. Childcare Information Service. OFSTED.

12. Similar approach. Consistency. Rewards. Positive reinforcement. Praise.

Further information

501 Ways to be a Good Parent by Michele Elliott (Hodder and Stoughton, 1996)

C14 Care for and promote the development of babies

This Unit covers baby care and development from six weeks to 12 months. It includes nutrition, physical care, stimulation and language development.

This chapter will enable you to:
C14.1 Provide for the nutritional needs of babies
C14.2 Manage the physical care of babies
C14.3 Promote the physical growth and development of babies
C14.4 Provide stimulation to foster the development of babies
C14.5 Promote the language development of babies.

Element C14.1 Provide for the nutritional needs of babies

➤ Your assessor can observe and question you. · · · · · · · · · · · · · · · · · · · **C14.1**: *range 1c* ◄

Finger food
Number of children: as appropriate.

Resources
Fresh foods, such as cheese, bread, eggs, vegetables and fruit.

Preparation
Check for any allergies or dietary requirements. Clean your hands and the babies', the surfaces and the food. Prepare finger foods, allowing food to cool.

What to do
➤ Grate some cheese and raw carrot, mix together and serve in a dish.
➤ Serve triangles of cheese on toast.
➤ Offer sticks of cooked carrot.
➤ Serve fingers of lightly buttered toast.
➤ Cut wedges of apple, lengths of bananas, slices of pear and avocado.
➤ Lengths of cucumber can soothe inflamed gums.
➤ Offer lightly cooked broccoli, cauliflower and potato.

Support and extension
Only give food the babies can cope with and always under strict supervision. Not all babies will like all the food offered. Introduce one new taste at a time. Discuss with parents the foods the babies are eating at home.

Tip

➤ Pesticides penetrate into the skin of fruit and vegetables. Wash off the surface dust and pesticide residue and peel for babies and toddlers.

C14.1: 6

➤ The energy intake required by a baby up to one year is 800 calories.

C14.1: 7

Evaluation

Did the babies enjoy experimenting with finger food? Did they swallow the food easily? Do you feel that any babies are ready to move on to new tastes?

Supporting activity

➤ **C14.1**: 6 · · · · · · · ·   Use the 'Menu sheet' photocopiable sheet on page 156 to draw up a baby ◄
menu. Ensure a balance of protein, fruit and vegetables, dairy and carbohydrates.

Case study

➤ **C14.1**: 1, 2, 3 · · · · ·   Daniel is two months old and his mother is returning to work, just down ◄
the road. She wants to continue breast feeding him, but she often has to visit clients. How will you advise her and how can you ensure Daniel's needs are met? Write down the case study with your responses for your portfolio.

Follow on

➤ **C14.1**: 11 · · · · · · ·   Good communication with parents is necessary when caring for babies ◄
and young children. To ensure consistency of care, consider how you can establish and maintain exchanges of information about babies' feeding patterns and intake, health and welfare. Share this information with your assessor.

Questions

(See answer pointers at end of chapter.)

➤ **C14.1**: 5 · · · · · · · ·   **1.** Describe your personal hygiene practices to minimise the spread of infection. ◄

➤ **C14.1**: 8 · · · · · · · ·   **2.** What temperature should milk be when given to the baby? When ◄
progressively weaning the baby what textures of food are appropriate?

➤ **C14.1**: 10 · · · · · · ·   **3.** Who are the special advisers you may call on in the care of babies and what ◄
can they advise on?

Record the questions and your full answers and share these with your assessor.

Did you know?

Research shows that of 1400 children born in 1991, by the age of two years a staggering 233 were overweight. By the age of four that figure had risen to 280. It has been estimated that 50 per cent of today's toddlers will become overweight as adults if current trends continue.

Extra idea

➤ **C14.1**: 4 · · · · · · · ·   Ensure feeding records are correct, legible and complete. Show your assessor. ◄

Element C14.2 Manage the physical care of babies

➤ Your assessor can observe and question you. · · · · · · · · · · · · · · ◄ **C14.2**: range 1a, b, 2a, b, 3a, b

Routines and practice
Number of children: one-to-one and group care.

Resources
Nursery and baby equipment; baby toys; clothing.

Preparation
Plan for each aspect of care as part of the regular routine.

What to do
➤ If babies cry, run through a simple checklist: are they hungry, thirsty, too hot or cold, need a nappy change, bored, tired, want a cuddle, anxious about leaving a parent, want attention, frustrated, teething, ill or hurt? Explain to your assessor how you judge the reason for crying.

➤ Ensure that milk and solid food is appropriate, frequent, satisfying for the baby and follows a satisfactory and hygienic routine.

➤ When changing nappies, ensure everything is ready. Interact with the baby and stay calm and unhurried. Safety and hygiene must have a high priority.

➤ When required, wash a baby and change all the necessary garments.

➤ Ensure that cots and mattresses meet current safety specifications and bedding is suitable, individual to the child and washed regularly.

➤ Ensure the indoor and outdoor play areas are safe. Note any potential hazards and the precautions to prevent accidents and cross-infection.

➤ Share with your assessor the selection criteria for choosing toys, from a health and safety perspective, and how to ensure their suitability for babies.

> ✔ **Tip**
>
> ➤ Babies need constant supervision due to their liability to fall, swallow unexpected objects, choke on food, be uncomfortable, because of changes in temperature, and because they may become ill very quickly.
>
> **C14.2**: 3

Support and extension
Organise activities specifically for the ages and abilities of the babies in your care. The equipment, toys and setting need to grow and develop with the babies.

Evaluation
➤ Did you demonstrate knowledge and understanding of why you undertook · · *Cross-reference to E3* ◄ activities, as well as being able to do them? Has it helped you to question why you do what you do? Do you feel better prepared to work with babies?

Supporting activity
Glue pictures of baby equipment in a montage. Write the names of the items and the safety features required around the edge. Include in your portfolio.

➤ **C14.2**: 8, 9 · · · · · ·

Case study

Tyo is nine months old and has been irritable over the last few days. His mother has taken him to the doctor and shows you a rash on his body, which the doctor thinks is due to an allergy, but is not sure what the cause is. Suggest possible internal and external reasons for the rash. Under what circumstances will you apply the cream the mother has brought in? Write down the case study with your responses for your portfolio.

Follow on

➤ **C14.2**: 9 · · · · · · ·

Consider, with babies in your care, what unusual conditions you would report to senior colleagues and parents. List the conditions that may cause concern.

Questions

(See answer pointers at end of chapter.)

➤ **C14.2**: 2 · · · · · · · ·

4. *Suggest safety features to consider when providing a cot and bedding.*

➤ **C14.2**: 2, 3, 4 · · · · ·

5. *Safety and hygiene play a large part in nappy changing and toilet training; describe the most important aspects.*

➤ **C14.2**: 8 · · · · · · · ·

6. *Describe what precautions must be taken before babies receive treatment or medicine?*

Record the questions and your full answers and share these with your assessor.

Did you know?

Experiments with orphaned baby rhesus monkeys demonstrated the need for comfort and affection. Two imitation 'mothers', one made of wire containing a feeding bottle and the other soft and padded, were placed in the monkey cage. The babies took the nourishment they needed from the wire 'mother', but once satisfied spent the rest of the time with the cuddly 'mother'. If they were not hungry they did not mind if the wire mother was removed, but became very distressed if the cuddly mother was taken away.

Extra idea

➤ **C14.2**: 10, cross- · · ·
reference **P2**

Keep a home–setting link book for each baby. At the time of an event, such as nappy changing, meals, feeding and sleeping, make a record. Share with the parent at the end of each day. The book can be used by parents to record overnight or weekend information they may wish to share.

Element C14.3 Promote the physical growth and development of babies

➤ **C14.3**: range 1a, b · ·

Your assessor can observe and question you.

Active games

Number of children: one-to-one or one-to-two.

Resources
Resources appropriate to the activity.

Preparation
Plan the activities using the 'Spider chart' photocopiable sheet on page 132. Write 'Active games' in the centre and a different game in each of the surrounding boxes, to be repeated over a two-week period.

Tip

➤ Remember that babies grow at different rates. Assess each one on its individual pattern of progress.

What to do
➤ Babies love to dance. Hold them upright, so they can sway and jiggle.
➤ Stitch bells to the babies' bootees, so they tinkle when kicking their feet.
➤ Encourage the babies to make noises with a wooden spoon and an old tin.
➤ During baths, invite the babies to catch and pop soap bubbles.
➤ Play 'Peek-a-boo' from behind a cloth, letting the babies take their turn.

➤ Use different-sized, coloured and textured balls to roll to one another.
➤ Use funny faces to communicate – whatever the baby does, you repeat it.
➤ On a warm day, mix cornflour and water and pour on a plastic sheet. Remove all the babies' clothes and let them play in the mixture.
➤ Provide large cardboard boxes that the babies can crawl through.

Support and extension
Once one game is mastered, try another that challenges the baby that little bit more. Babies will soon let you know if they are bored.

Evaluation
Did the activities encourage interaction, new skills and physical involvement? Did the babies want to repeat any activities? Did any activities cause you concern? Which will you repeat?

Supporting activity
➤ Let the babies post and retrieve familiar toys from a box. Record your findings on the 'Baby development and stimulation chart' photocopiable sheet on page 155. Note the approaches of different babies.

Cross-reference to **C16** ◄

Case study
➤ Ten-month-old twins, Robert and Bethan, live in an overcrowded flat with their mum and three older siblings. There is little room for them to move freely and their mum is delighted with the nursery as it has a garden. How can you make the most of the outdoor play space to enable the twins to fully utilise it? Write down the case study with your responses for your portfolio.

C14.3: 2, 3, 4, 6, 7, 8 ◄

➤ **C14.3**: *4, 5* · · · · · · ·

Follow on

Twins may have a low birth weight and take time to catch up emotionally and developmentally. Find out how you can support twins and their parents. Visit the Twins and Multiple Births Association website: www.tamba.org.uk ◄

Questions

(See answer pointers at end of chapter.)

➤ **C14.3**: *1* · · · · · · · · **7.** *Suggest games and materials to develop hand–eye co-ordination in babies.* ◄

➤ **C14.3**: *3* · · · · · · · **8.** *What opportunities can you suggest for non-mobile babies to gain exercise?* ◄

➤ **C14.3**: *8* · · · · · · **9.** *What safety features for mobile babies would you expect in a home setting?* ◄

Record the questions and your full answers and share these with your assessor.

Did you know?

At birth, babies heads account for 25 per cent of their length and 33 per cent of their bodies' volume. The head circumference at birth is larger than the chest, but by the first birthday they are about the same.

Extra idea

➤ **C14.3**: *6* · · · · · · · · Toys for babies need to be safe and hygienic. Show your assessor the criteria ◄ you use to select suitable toys and how and when you maintain them.

Element C14.4 Provide stimulation to foster the development of babies

➤ **C14.4**: *range 1b,* · · · · Your assessor can observe and question you. ◄
c, 2a

Printing for babies

Number of children: one-to-one or one-to-two.

Resources

Ready-mixed, non-toxic paint in bright colours; sugar paper; plates; commercial, shaped print sponges and applicators; small boxes and tubes in an appropriate size for the babies to grip; items suitable for printing; aprons; liquid soap; kitchen roll; towel; table cover; bowl.

Preparation

Plan the activity using the 'Activity plan' photocopiable sheet on page 131. Dress the babies in coverall aprons. Cover the table or use a high chair that can be washed. Fill the bowl with warm soapy water. Using two colours of paint, squeeze each into separate plates, just enough to cover the bottom.

What to do

➤ This is a fun activity with a purpose. Babies learn through doing, feeling, manipulating and looking. The benefits are in the experience, not the finished product. Try the following printing activities at different times.

➤ Use different-sized and coloured papers in different locations.
➤ Hand printing is always good fun.
➤ Use commercial printing sponges and applicators with good grips.
➤ Print circles using cardboard tubes or lengths of foam pipe insulation.
➤ Use commercial sponge paint rollers for an instant and effective result.
➤ Print with eggcups, fabric, plastic toys or other small items.
➤ Display the babies' prints around photos of the babies doing the printing.

Support and extension
Introduce young babies to printing while sitting in a highchair and use a low table for mobile children.

Evaluation
What safety aspects did you consider before presenting these activities? Can you identify the learning experiences gained? Were enough adults involved to ensure adequate supervision? Did you choose the right location for the activity?

Supporting activity
➤ Make a list of other hands-on activities the babies can experience. Suggest · · **C14.4**: 2 ◄
how to present these and what safety factors need to be considered.

Case study
➤ Nine-month-old Fran had a difficult birth, resulting in a blood clot in her brain. She made a good recovery, but has a weakness in her left hand and a slight delay in her intellectual development. With stimulation and exercise, she is expected to recover fully. Suggest activities for the next three months. Write down the case study with your responses for your portfolio.

C14.4: 1, 2, 3, 4, 6, ◄
7, 9

Follow on
➤ Complete the 'Baby development and stimulation chart' photocopiable sheet on page 155 for three age groups: four months, eight months and 12 months. Write in the average developmental level that you would expect under the headings and suggest suitable activities in the final box.

C14.4: 2, 3, 4, ◄
C14.3: 3

Questions
(See answer pointers at end of chapter.)
➤ **10.** *How can you ensure the environment is safe for babies to explore?* · · · · · **C14.4**: 1 ◄
➤ **11.** *Which parts of the daily routine provide opportunities for play, interaction* · · **C14.4**: 3 ◄
and sensory experiences?
➤ **12.** *How can you encourage parents to be involved in their child's play?* · · · · · **C14.4**: 9 ◄

Record the questions and your full answers and share these with your assessor.

Did you know?
Native American babies were traditionally strapped to a cradle board in their first year. However, when released, they quickly caught up with other children.

Tip
➤ Be selective with baby toys. Sort them out into assorted activities and place in boxes. Bring one box out at a time. The next day or at the next playtime, bring out a different one.

C14.4: 2

Extra idea
Babies need stimulating play in the same way children do. Ensure you offer a balance of physical, creative, imaginative and intellectual play.

Element C14.5 Promote the language development of babies

➤ **C14.5**: range 1a, b · · · Your assessor can question you.   ◄

Mobiles to talk about
Number of children: whole group.

Resources
Two metal coat-hangers or two rulers; brightly coloured ribbon; nylon fishing line; darning needle; assortment of materials for hanging on the mobile, such as card, tinsel, Cellophane, old greeting cards, cardboard tubes, small empty boxes, wrapping paper, bright or shiny small toys; paint; glue; sticky tape; stapler; ceiling hook.

Preparation
Prepare using the 'Spider chart' photocopiable sheet on page 132. Write 'Mobile' in the centre and the reasons for making the mobile in the boxes.

What to do
➤ Tie the coat-hangers at cross-angles with ribbon, leaving some dangling.
➤ Wrap the ribbon over the coat-hangers to cover them.
➤ Choose objects to hang from the mobile, such as parcels and ribbons, bunches of shiny Cellophane or a collection of small toys.
➤ Do not use small parts that can drop off and be picked up by the babies. Ensure everything is firmly attached and check regularly.
➤ Thread the fishing line through the hanging shape and tie the other end securely to the coat-hangers. Ensure the hangings can move and twirl.
➤ Hang from a ceiling hook, so that the mobile is just above adult head height if in the open room, or lower, but out of reach, if over a cot.

✓ **Tip**
➤ Make sure there are no dangling ribbons or ties within reach of the baby at any time.

Support and extension
Draw younger babies attention to the mobile, talk about it, make it move, describe the colours, shapes and features. Change the objects now and again.

Evaluation
Did the babies smile at the mobile? Did they respond when you talked to them? Did you keep drawing their attention to the mobile?

Supporting activity
➤ **C14.5**: 3, cross-· · · Make a collection of baby rhymes and songs, lullabies, simple nursery rhymes ◄
reference to **C11**   and action songs. Collect props to illustrate the songs in a bag. The babies will soon recognise the props as well as the songs, adding another dimension.

Case study

➤ Oliver's father never speaks to him when he picks him up from the setting. You hear him tell another father that there is no point talking to a baby as they cannot understand. How can you persuade Oliver's dad of the importance of talking to babies? What strategies can you suggest? Write down the case study with your responses for your portfolio.

C14.5: *1, 2, 3, 4, 6, 7, 8* ◄

Follow on

➤ Note the interaction parents and carers have with the babies. Be aware as to whether babies respond consistently in a particular way to some people.

C14.5: *7* ◄

Questions
(See answer pointers at end of chapter.)

➤ **13.** *In what ways can you develop listening skills in a baby?* · · · · · · · · · · · **C14.5**: *4* ◄
➤ **14.** *What forms of non-verbal communication do babies use?* · · · · · · · · · **C14.5**: *5* ◄
➤ **15.** *How can you encourage and reinforce babies' attempts to communicate?* · · **C14.5**: *7, 8* ◄

Record the questions and your full answers and share these with your assessor.

Did you know?

A young baby cannot speak, but the importance of language in the earliest days, cannot be underestimated: 'It is very important to talk to your baby. If you or your family speak another language do use it to speak to your baby. It can give your child a head start, such as learning other languages, and help them to enjoy another culture'. *(The Pregnancy Book,* NHS, 2001)

Extra idea

➤ Let the babies use a toy telephone to encourage speech. Write a reflective · · **C14.5**: *6, 7* ◄
account of how, when and how often babies use this for listening and talking.

Practical ways of collecting evidence
Use a tape recorder to both collect evidence of speech and language development and to intrigue the children by offering recorded familiar sounds.

Check your progress
This Unit covers all aspects of caring for babies. It is expected that you will be directly observed by your assessor for at least one aspect of each of the range statements for each of the five Elements in this Unit. You may be observed for more, but if you have not, then you need to collect evidence by other means. This can be by reflective accounts, inspection of the setting, work products, child observations and witness testimonies. Most of the evidence will be part of the normal routine and care, additional items are suggested here to include extra stimulation and discovery.

Answer pointers

Ensure your answers are fully made for your assessor.

1. Wash hands. Clean surfaces. Boil water. Store in fridge. Covering teat. Wear apron.

2. Body temperature. Cool. Sieve. Mash. Process. Chop. Whisk. Finger food.

3. Midwife. General Practitioner. Health Visitor. Paediatrician. Feeding. Sleeping. Development. Special needs. Concerns.

4. Safe. Firm and snug mattress. Bars between 25mm and 60mm. Moving parts work smoothly. No cot bumpers. No ties. British Standard 1753. No duvets or quilts.

5. Wash hands. Wear apron and gloves. Clean baby. Girls front to back. Nappy disposal. Bin or bucket. Out of reach. Own potty. Sterilise. Wash hands.

6. Prescribed. Follow instructions. Written permission. Procedures. Own sun cream. Specific plans.

7. Balls. Crayons. Pull along toys. Posting boxes. Rattles. Hammer peg toys. Clothes pegs and a container.

8. Kicking. Splashing in the bath. 'Riding' on an adult's leg. Bouncing on adult's lap. Supported 'walking'. Clapping. Baby bouncers. Banging toys. Bouncing cradles.

9. Stair gate. Cupboard locks. Highchair harness. Door stops. Fire guards. Pram brakes.

10. Clean. Secure. No hazards. Appropriate toys. No small pieces. No broken toys. No long strings or ribbons. Doors. Non-toxic. Suitable flooring. Toys within reach.

11. Meal times. Nappy changing. Bath time. Play time. Going for a walk. Shopping. Meeting people. Cuddling. Massaging.

12. Keep them informed. Join in. Support. Demonstrate. Observe others. Join a parent and baby group.

13. Whispering. Waiting. Singing. Rhythmic chanting. Talking. Making sounds with toys. Pointing out sounds. Tone and pitch of voice. Reduce distractions.

14. Tongue responses. Eye contact. Crying. Laughing. Posture. Facial expression. Body language. Gestures.

15. Verbal turn-taking. Talking and listening. Singing. Repeating baby sounds. Show pleasure. Interpret.

Further information

The ABC of Healthy Eating for Babies and Toddlers by Jeanette Marshall (Hodder & Stoughton, 1997)

Baby Wisdom by Deborah Jackson (Hodder & Stoughton, 2002)

C17 Promote the care and education of children with special needs

This Unit covers working with children with degrees of physical, sensory, intellectual and communication impairment as well as behavioural or emotional difficulties. It includes activities, specialist equipment, working with parents and integrating children into mainstream provision and the community.

This Unit will enable you to:
C17.1 Enable children with special needs to participate in activities
C17.2 Support parents to respond to the special needs of their children
C17.3 Contribute to the use of specialist equipment
C17.4 Communicate with children with special needs
C17.5 Contribute to the inclusion of children with special needs.

Element C17.1 Enable children with special needs to participate in activities

➤ Your assessor can observe and question you. · · · · · · · · · · · · · · · · · **C17.1**: range 1a, b ◀

Tactile trails

Number of children: small groups at a time; whole group creation.

Resources

Border paper or card about 60mm wide and as long as you want the trail to be; 100mm circles cut from sugar paper or card; glue; spreaders; stapler; staple gun or Blu-Tack; assortment of textured collage materials, such as cotton-wool balls, chopped yarn or string, shredded paper, scrunched Cellophane, scraps of fabric, small pasta, leaves, aluminium foil, sand, wood shavings, dried herbs and glitter.

Preparation

Plan the activity using the 'Activity plan' photocopiable sheet on page 131. Put the collage materials into separate containers. Provide several circles for each child. Put out glue and spreaders for everyone.

What to do

➤ Pass the containers around so the children can feel, smell and see the contents. Introduce new words, such as 'texture', 'aromatic' and 'Cellophane'.

 Tip

➤ Remember the child comes first and the disability afterwards.

C17.1: 7

➤ Show your assessor how progress records for children with special needs are completed in your setting.

C17.1: 8

➤ Let the children choose their materials and glue them to the circles.

➤ Keep the materials on a tray for visually impaired children, so they do not move out of reach.

➤ Ask the children where the border should be placed. It is best to fix it at child level, along a wall, without obstruction, and leading from one point of interest to another, such as the book corner to the lunch boxes.

➤ Staple the circles along the centre of the border, touching edge to edge.

➤ Attach the completed border to the wall with a staple gun or Blu-Tack.

➤ Encourage the children to follow the line round by gently feeling along it.

Support and extension

➤ *Cross-reference to*
C3, **C10**

Some children may need help with one circle, while others will be able to complete several.   ◀

Evaluation

How do you feel the activity went? Were all the children able to participate? Was any child bored? Did you introduce new words? Did you praise the children to encourage them? Was the end result fun, satisfying and useful?

Supporting activity

➤ **C17.1**: *1, 4, cross-reference* **E3**

Assess your setting to see how user friendly it is for children with special   ◀
needs. Can a child with mobility difficulties move easily around the setting? Are coat pegs distinctive enough for a visually impaired child to recognise by touch? Is there a coloured line to follow to the cloakroom on the wall or floor? Note any other relevant features. Record your findings for your portfolio.

Case study

➤ **C17.1**: *2, 3, 5*

The left side of Matthew's body is affected by cerebral palsy. He wears a   ◀
calliper on his left leg and has a splint on his left hand and arm. However, Matthew is in a mainstream school and particularly likes sports and games. How can you help Matthew to fully participate in sports and games? Write down the case study with your responses for your portfolio.

Follow on

Consider the implications of cerebral palsy and the long-term impact of the condition. Look at relevant websites, such as: www.scope.org.uk, www.mynchen.demon.co.uk and www.ashadeep.net

Questions

(See answer pointers at end of chapter.)

➤ **C17.1**: *2*   **1.** *Suggest games for a child using a wheelchair with the use of only one hand.*   ◀

➤ **C17.1**: *3*   **2.** *Describe a variety of specialist equipment, adaptations and aids you are*   ◀
aware of to help children with special needs to fully participate in activities.

➤ **C17.1**: *6*   **3.** *What factors dictate the length of time a child with special needs should*   ◀
spend on any particular activity?

Record the questions and your full answers and share these with your assessor.

Did you know?

Glue ear is the single greatest cause of hearing loss in children. If not diagnosed and treated early on, it affects hearing and speech, as well as learning and can contribute to behavioural difficulties.

Extra idea

➤ Talk to a paediatric occupational therapist about equipment available for · · · · **C17.1**: *3* ◄
children with special needs. Investigate websites: www.taylortherapy.co.uk,
www.romamedical.co.uk, www.jenx.com and www.algeos.com

Element C17.2 Support parents to respond to the special needs of their children

➤ Your assessor can observe you interacting with parents and question you. · · · · · **C17.2**: *range 1a, b, c,* ◄
2a, b

Including the parents

Number of children: all, or as appropriate.

Resources

Any additional resources a particular child with special needs may require.

What to do

➤ Encourage parents and practitioners to share information and advice.
➤ Ask parents how best to communicate with their child, for example, facing a deaf child and not standing with the light behind you.
➤ Consult parents and children if an Individual Learning Programme is set up.
➤ Find out from and share with parents any special tips to help, such as giving a child with Autism a particular carpet square to sit on.
➤ Invite parents to all meetings about their children.
➤ Use a home–setting link book to inform practitioners and parents of issues.
➤ Discuss specialist terms and medication requirements with parents.
➤ Consider parents for whom English is a second language and what the best means of communicating information may be.
➤ Parents may have a disability or difficulty. Ensure they have access to the setting and you are able to communicate with them.
➤ Working with parents is a two-way process. You can support and advise them, and they can help and advise you on the care of their child.

Support and extension

You will need to adapt your interaction for each individual situation. There are times you will need to communicate with parents more frequently, particularly when the child is new to the setting.

✔ **Tip**

➤ Always remember parents are *the* experts on their own child.

Evaluation

Are the setting policies and systems for interacting with parents appropriate and adequate? Is there opportunity for you to regularly communicate with parents of children with special needs? How else can you involve parents?

Supporting activity

➤ **C17.2**: 2, 5, 6, 8 · · ·   Read all the setting's policies and highlight the references to parents. If you do ◄ not feel there is sufficient detail relating to parents then write additional ones of your own. Discuss with your assessor, who may question you on them.

➤ **C17.2**: 4, 5, 6, 8 · · ·
Case study

Patrick developed leukaemia and missed a great deal of his Reception class due to his treatment. His parents are anxious about his health and education. Patrick is now in remission and behaves much like any other five-year-old. However, his parents are inclined to be over cautious and restrict his activities. How can you help them adjust, reassure them and work with them to support Patrick? Write down the case study with your responses for your portfolio.

Follow on

➤ **C17.2**: 3 · · · · · · ·   Find out about anaemia, leukaemia, thalassaemia and sickle cell anaemia – what the symptoms are, the treatment and the prognosis.

Questions

(See answer pointers at end of chapter.)

➤ **C17.2**: 1 · · · · · · ·   **4.** *How can you ensure that information you give to parents is accurate, up to* ◄ *date and consistent with care and education plans?*

➤ **C17.2**: 2 · · · · · · ·   **5.** *Who do you consider are the relevant individuals who have responsibility to* ◄ *inform and support parents if it is beyond your role?*

➤ **C17.2**: 7 · · · · · · ·   **6.** *If you find a particular strategy works what can you do with that knowledge?* ◄

Record the questions and your full answers and share these with your assessor.

Did you know?

Not all disabilities and special needs are readily visible. Children may have epilepsy, grand mal or petit mal, heart conditions, emotional disturbances, hearing loss or other conditions that are not visually obvious.

Extra ideas

Use the Internet to update your knowledge and share with the parents. Some useful websites to check are: www.cafamily.org.uk, www.familyonwards.com and www.childrenwithdisabilities.ncjrs.org

If parents are not confident using this medium, show them how to get the information either in the setting or in the local library. Your assessor can observe you working with the parents, or the parents can give you a witness testimony.

Element C17.3 Contribute to the use of specialist equipment

➤ Your assessor can observe and question you. · · · · · · · · · · · · · · · · · · · ◄ *C17.3*: range *1a, b, c, d, 2a, b, c*

Finding the information

Number of children: as appropriate to individual children.

What to do

➤ Ensure you can recognise the signs and characteristics to indicate hearing impairment in a baby. Study a child development manual.

➤ In order to recognise difficulties affecting vision, you need to know what to expect in the range of development for young children.

➤ Parents usually know much, about their child and their conditions.

➤ Contact your local Disability Officer to find out about services in your area.

➤ Parents may benefit from parental support groups. Being in touch with another family in a similar situation can be mutually supportive.

➤ Make a list of the specialists involved with children in your setting – who they are, where they can be contacted and what they do.

➤ Encourage parents to communicate with their local Disability Officer, as they are responsibile for providing services and planning for future services.

➤ The Citizens Advice Bureau or the local Social Security Department will advise you on the benefits available to support children with special needs.

➤ Each setting will have a special needs policy and access to a Special Needs Co-ordinator (SENCO).

✔ **Tip**

➤ Ensure the layout of the room is well thought out to maximise the child's ability to participate.

C17.3: 2

Support and extension

As you find more ways of gaining information and knowledge, keep a note of sources for future reference.

Evaluation

Have you gained specific as well as general knowlege on special needs and equipment? Have you talked to colleagues, specialists and other professionals? Have you listened to parents? Have the children taught you anything new?

Supporting activity

➤ Keep a reference box file containing leaflets and booklets about conditions, · · *C17.3*: 3 ◄
equipment and services to share with parents.

Case study

➤ Since coming to the setting six months ago, Macey's mobility has improved, her social skills have increased and most of the time she is content. However she is frustrated by her fine motor skills and grip. She tires easily, finds drawing and mark making difficult and has to be helped to eat. What specialist equipment can you suggest that Macey uses to help her progress in this area? Write down the case study with your responses for your portfolio.

C17.3: 3, 5, 6 ◄

➤ **C17.3**: 1 · · · · · · ·
> **Follow on**
> Many early years catalogues carry a small range of equipment specially designed to address particular difficulties. See if you can find any. Contact or visit organisations involved with children with special needs to assess the range and variety of aids to everyday living that are available. ◄

Questions
(See answer pointers at end of chapter.)

➤ **C17.3**: 5, 8 · · · · · · **7.** In the interests of the child, what do you need to be aware of when ensuring ◄ aids are applied, fitted and used?

➤ **C17.3**: 6 · · · · · · · **8.** How can you ensure appropriate care for an incontinent child? What ◄ specialist equipment can be used?

➤ **C17.3**: 7, 9 · · · · · · **9.** What will you do if you notice defects in equipment or discomfort in its use? ◄

Record the questions and your full answers and share these with your assessor.

> **Did you know?**
> The National Parent Partnership Network provides support for parents of children with special needs.
> Visit: www.parentpartnership.org.uk

Extra idea

➤ **C17.3**: 2, 3, 7 · · · · · Widen your awareness of the use of specialist equipment by spending some ◄ time in a specialist school.

Element C17.4 Communicate with children with special needs

➤ **C17.4**: range 1a, · · · Your assessor can observe and question you. ◄
b, c, 2a, b, c, d

Communication games
Number of children: four to whole group.

Resources
Resources appropriate to the chosen activity.

Preparation
Plan the activity chosen using the 'Activity plan' photocopiable sheet on page 131. Prepare according to the chosen activity.

What to do
➤ Encourage children to act out situations using body language.
➤ Teach all the children simple nursery rhymes in Makaton signing system.

➤ Cut pictures from magazines that imply an instruction, such as 'sit down' or 'stand up', and glue to individual cards. When you want the children to respond show them the appropriate picture. Always use the same card with the same instruction, so the children get to know what is expected of them.
➤ Try using puppets to speak through to aid communication.
➤ Give a pair of children two cards, with 'Yes' and 'No' on. Let the children ask each other questions, that can only be answered with the cards.
➤ Gently throw a beanbag to each child in turn. Explain that this indicates it is their turn to communicate and everyone else will listen.

Tip

➤ Children with communication difficulties or special needs may have low self-esteem. Give lots of praise and encouragement and use activities that boost their self-image.

Support and extension

Ensure activities are related to age and ability and are inclusive. Communication is about talking/communicating and listening/interpreting. Simplify or vary the games to make them easier or more complex as appropriate.

Evaluation

Which activities worked best? Suggest other ways to practise communication? Do you use specialist communication equipment? Can you use it more imaginatively? Did you join in? Did you need an interpreter? Was it fun?

Supporting activity

➤ Make a collection of rhymes or sayings that address difficulties with particular sounds, such as, 'Sammy snake slithers and slides sss... sss... sss...', for a child having difficulty with the S sound. Use these at rhyme time with the group.

C17.4: 1, 3 ◄

Case study

➤ Scarlet is 15 months old and profoundly deaf. She wears a hearing aid in a harness strapped to her chest. How can you prepare yourself, Scarlet, her parents and the other children for this new experience? Write down the case study with your responses for your portfolio.

C17.4: 1, 2, 3, 4, 5, 6, ◄ 7

Follow on

➤ Consider taking a course in British Sign Language or a Makaton language programme. Look at websites for further information, including: www.foot-print.demon.co.uk and www.makaton.org

C17.4: range 1c ◄

Questions

(See answer pointers at end of chapter.)
➤ **10.** *What are the different methods a child may use to communicate?* · · · · · **C17.4**: 1, 5 ◄
➤ **11.** *Who are the communication specialists that work with your setting?* · · · · **C17.4**: 4 ◄
➤ **12.** *How will you answer the children's questions about other children's aids?* · · **C17.4**: 6 ◄

Record the questions and your full answers and share these with your assessor.

Did you know?
Every week 200 babies are born in the United Kingdom with a learning disability. Older first-time mothers have a higher risk of having a child with a developmental problem.

➤ **C17.4**: 2 · · · · · · · · ·

Extra idea
Invite a child to copy an asymmetrical pattern. Pass their copy to the next ◄ child to study for a few seconds. Ask the second child to draw the pattern from memory. Continue, until everyone has had a turn. Compare the first and last drawings to see how the pattern has changed.

Element C17.5 Contribute to the inclusion of children with special needs

➤ **C17.5**: *range 1a,* · · ·
   2b

It is not required that you should be directly observed for this Element. It can ◄ be cross-referenced into other Units.

Play with natural materials
Number of children: individual or small groups.

Resources
Silver sand; shallow tray; sand tray; twice-washed sand; outdoor sand box or tractor tyre; different-sized containers; spoons; buckets and spades; water; water toys; paint; small play toys; natural materials; small cardboard boxes; sequins; coconut fibre; plastic sheeting; water tray or other containers; other appropriate resources from around the setting; aprons; sand hats.

✓ Tip

➤ Observations of children with special needs, as part of a research process, show that the children are more likely to spend more time looking, listening and waiting than their peers.

Preparation
Plan the activity using the 'Activity plan' photocopiable sheet on page 131. Prepare according to the chosen activity.

What to do
➤ Sand is a soothing material and presents a valuable learning experience. Offer the children tools and equipment to promote mathematical learning.
➤ Select tools and equipment to develop the children's scientific skills.
➤ Make sand more interesting by adding paint to water and mixing it in.
➤ Instead of sand, offer sterilised coconut fibre from a garden centre on plastic sheeting on the floor. This is particularly good for dinosaurs!
➤ Present the water in different-shaped and sized containers; colour the water; supply fish and boats; provide equipment for scientific experiments; promote mathematical concepts; use bubbles, providing no one is allergic.

Support and extension

➤ *Cross-reference to* · · ·
   C10

Less able children may need an adult to help and some may only be able to ◄ experience the sand and water being trickled over their hands or legs. More able children can develop the activities to their level of ability.

Evaluation

Could all the children join in? Did some need aids to access the activity? Did you have the right aids? Can you provide these next time? Did you offer the right amount of stimulation? What else could you use? Did learning take place? Did you use appropriate mathematical and scientific words?

Supporting activity

➤ Plan a trip to a local swimming pool. Establish how to get there, assess the access, the toilet facilities, how many adults you will need and any other considerations. Share your ideas with your assessor and put in your portfolio.

C17.5: 6, cross-reference to *E3* ◄

Case study

➤ Two-year-old twins, Freddie and George, are starting soon. Freddie has Downs Syndrome. How can you explain to a new practitioner the qualities that make a setting inclusive, to benefit Freddie and George. Write down the case study with your responses for your portfolio.

C14.5: 2, 4, 5 ◄

Follow on

➤ Investigate the pros and cons of exclusive special needs settings and inclusive mainstream settings. Write up your findings and discuss with your assessor.

C17.5: 3, 7 ◄

Questions

(See answer pointers at end of chapter.)

➤ **13.** *In what ways can you promote inclusion in the local community?* · · · · · · · *C17.5*: 1, 3 ◄

➤ **14.** *What support can you give parents to make use of inclusion opportunities?* — *C17.5*: 4 ◄

➤ **15.** *Describe your role in relation to children with special needs. Record in what* *C17.5*: 7, 8 ◄
circumstances and with whom you would refer issues on.

Record the questions and your full answers and share these with your assessor.

Did you know?

Article 23.1 in the United Nations Convention on the Rights of the Child states: 'Parties recognize that a mentally or physically disabled child should enjoy a full and decent life, in conditions which ensure dignity, promote self-reliance, and facilitate the child's active participation in the community'.

Extra idea

➤ Read books relating to children with special needs and answer children's · · · *C17.5*: 2 ◄
questions simply but honestly.

Practical ways of collecting evidence

Your assessor will directly observe how you communicate with parents and children. It may not be necessary to arrange any particular activities, however, playing a communication game may give evidence for different Elements in the Unit. Working on a holistic basis, where one piece of evidence fulfils a number of performance criteria, is the most effective way to work.

Check your progress
You are expected to be directly observed in at least one of the range statements of all the Elements, with the exception of **C17.5**. In mainstream provision it can be difficult collecting some evidence, particularly relating to specialist equipment. If children in your setting do not use the equipment specified, your assessor will observe you working with what you have. You may have to gain some experience in another setting for a short time to be directly observed, to fulfil the requirements of the Standards.

Answer pointers
Ensure your answers are fully made for your assessor.
1. Beanbags. Table-top toys. Jigsaws. Peg boards. Magnetic games. Play dough. Board games. Crayoning.
2. Hearing aid. Glasses. Callipers. Splints. Walking frames. Loop system. Crutches. Pencil grips. Feeder beakers.
3. Attention span. Interest. Routine. Medical condition. Concentration. Comfort level. Fatigue.
4. Use current information. Ask parents. Ask colleagues. Check with professionals. Use the Internet. Read articles. Check Individual Learning Programmes regularly.
5. Senior colleagues. Paediatrician. Specialist nurse. Physiotherapist. Teaching staff.
6. Share with parents and colleagues. Demonstrate. Record. Keep notes.
7. Self-help. Comfortable. Applied correctly. Clean. Dignity. Privacy. Safe.
8. Diet. Privacy. Sensitively. Pads. Efficiently. Bags. Fluid intake. Parental advice. Catheters. Nappies. Waterproofs. Plastic pants.
9. Report. Inform colleagues. Parents. Occupational therapist. Child.
10. Signing. Oral. Keyboards. Tactile. Written. Phonic pack. Makaton.
11. Speech therapist. Specialist teachers. Workers from specialist voluntary organisations. Audiologist. Community Medical Officers.
12. Sensitively. Promptly. Honestly. Explain. Involve. Positively.
13. Special needs agencies. Visiting. Parents' groups. Inviting in visitors.
14. Welcome in. Support group. Advice. Information. Meetings with professionals. Demonstrations. Encouragement. Sharing skills.
15. Colleague. Occupational therapist. SENCO. Health Visitor. Paediatrician.

Further information
www.conductive-education.org.uk
www.leukaemiasociety.org

For contact addresses on childhood diseases and services:
www.londonhealth.co.uk/children.asp
www.mencap.org.uk

C24 Support the development of children's literacy skills

The focus of this Unit is on supporting teachers in their implementation of literacy skills; reading, comprehension and writing. This Unit is appropriate for practitioners in all settings where children are supported individually or in groups, especially those who support teachers at Key Stage 1 or its equivalent.

This chapter will enable you to:
C24.1 Help develop children's reading skills
C24.2 Help develop children's comprehension skills
C24.3 Help develop children's writing skills.

Element C24.1 Help develop children's reading skills

➤ Your assessor can observe and question you. · · · · · · · · · · · · · · ➤ *C24.1: range 1a, b, 2a, b, 3a, b, c* ◄

Creating a personal reading book
Number of children: six.

Resources
Sheets of A3 paper; one sheet of coloured A3 card; pencils; ruler; A5 paper; magazines and catalogues; scissors; glue; photos; long arm stapler.

Preparation
Plan the activity using the 'Activity plan' photocopiable sheet on page 131. Place the A3 paper and card together and fold down the centre to make a book. Staple together. Draw a line near the bottom of the page to write on.

What to do
➤ Ask the children to make up their own story from personal experiences.
➤ Invite the children to draw pictures to tell their story. Help them sort the pictures into an order. For example, some furniture representing 'my bedroom'.
➤ Help the children to cut the pictures out and stick them on the page.
➤ Encourage children to write a word or sentence at the bottom of the page.
➤ Make the books dual language with the help of a translator.
➤ Start with two or three pages, adding extra pages on subsequent days.
➤ Encourage the children to read the words from the first page, using the conventions of left to right and correct sentence structure. Discuss the illustrations together, turn over and repeat, until you come to the end.
➤ Write a list of the words in the book on the back page as they are added.

> Encourage the children to read some familiar and unfamiliar material every day.

C24.1: *1, 2*

> Children need to be heard reading in order to support and encourage them to gain confidence.

C24.1: *6, 7*

Support and extension

Scribe single noun words initially, such as 'bed' with less experienced children. Develop this to 'my bedroom' and 'the bed in my bedroom is red' with more experienced children. Write what the children choose as it is *their* book.

Evaluation

Did the children follow instruction? Could they read the words? Can you develop this idea further? Can parents help work with the children? Can parents do this at home with their children?

Supporting activity

Conduct an audit on reading opportunities in your setting. Identify the range of texts available for the children to read. Look at the book selection, labels, displays and workbooks. Look at corridors, notice boards and setting signs.

> **C24.1**: *2, 5, 6, 7, 8*

Case study

Marcel has suddenly realised that the strange squiggles he sees in books, on posters and on cereal boxes, actually have meaning. Routine activities take a long time as he stops all the time to ask you what this letter or word means, or attempts to read it to you. How can you help develop this one stage further? Write down the case study with your responses for your portfolio.

Follow on

> *Cross-reference to* **C3**, **C5**, **C10**

Assess the transferable skills you see children using in routine play situations. Identify ones that develop fine motor skills, hand–eye co-ordination, picture recognition, recognition of shape and symbol, intellect and self-esteem.

Questions

(See answer pointers at end of chapter.)

> **C24.1**: *3, 4*
> **C24.1**: *5*
> **C24.1**: *9*

1. *How can you ensure children are receptive to read and use reading conventions?*
2. *What cues encourage children to understand text and increase comprehension?*
3. *What is meant by the structure of the text, which children need to learn to be able to read accurately, fluently and with expression?*

Record the questions and your full answers and share these with your assessor.

Did you know?

There are over four and a half thousand public libraries in the United Kingdom, with over 17 million active users. About three and a half million books are issued to children every year, of these, 83 per cent are fiction and 17 per cent are non-fiction.

Extra idea

> **C24.1**

Your assessor can directly observe you listening to children read, supporting and encouraging them, and recording the results.

Element C24.2 Help develop children's comprehension skills

➤ Your assessor can observe and question you. · · · · · · · · · · · · · · · **C24.2**: *range 1, 2b, 3a, 4a, 5c* ◄

Traditional stories
Number of children: small group.

Resources
Any traditional story, such as 'Goldilocks and the Three Bears'.

Preparation
Familiarise yourself with the story until you are comfortable telling it.

What to do
➤ Read the story to the children straight through from beginning to end.
➤ Read the story a second time, discussing the pictures with the children.
➤ Talk about the issues and experiences raised: going into someone else's house; eating their food; sleeping in someone else's bed; running away.
➤ The next day, discuss the story and encourage the children to re-tell it.
➤ Ask the children to remember what happens, the order and the issues.
➤ Talk about the content and how the children think the characters felt.
➤ Ask if they can invent a new character for the story. What will happen?
➤ Ask the children to change the ending and predict subsequent events.

✓ **Tip**
➤ Whatever a child's actual age, choose activities at their reading level age.

Support and extension
Choose a simple familiar story to read to younger children. Offer older children less familiar or more complex stories.

Evaluation
Did you feel confident telling the story? Did the children remember the story and the sequence of events? Could they follow the reasoning in the story? Were they comfortable giving their views? Did they understand what to do?

Supporting activity
➤ Use different media for story-telling, such as videos, puppets, drama and · · · **C24.2**: *2, 3, 4, 7, 8* ◄
computers. Find out which ones the children understand and prefer.

Case study
➤ A year ago Ishmael could not speak English. He is now beginning to string words together. However, you are not sure about his ability to comprehend complex situations. You decide to read a poem and quiz the children afterwards to see if they understand and remember events. How will you know if Ishmael comprehends the complexities and how can you judge his progress? Write down the case study with your responses for your portfolio.

C24.2: *2, 7, 9, 10* ◄

➤ *Cross-reference to*
C11

Follow on

Consider whether the books in your setting cover a variety of stories and non-fiction situations that will encourage children to read, not only with fluency, but also with the understanding required to appreciate the nuances.

Questions

(See answer pointers at end of chapter.)

➤ **C24.2**: *1* · · · · · · · **4.** *How do you judge a child's comprehension skills? How can you build on them?* ◄

➤ **C24.2**: *5* · · · · · · · **5.** *What sort of reading material will encourage a child to read effectively?* ◄

➤ **C24.2**: *6* · · · · · · · **6.** *How can you encourage children to select their own reading materials?* ◄

Record the questions and your full answers and share these with your assessor.

Did you know?

Many English words have their origins in other languages. This can make it difficult to explain to children some of the irregularities, such as the silent 'g' in sign (Latin), 'k' in knee (German) and 'w' in wrong (Scandinavian).

Extra idea

➤ **C24.2**: *3* · · · · · · · Cut a sheet of A4 paper in half lengthwise. Create a concertina with one half. ◄ Fold the paper in half, keeping the fold towards you. Fold both paper edges back to meet at the centre. Copy 'The story of the snowman' photocopiable sheet on page 157. Ask the children to colour it in. Cut out the squares and glue them in sequence on each fold, on one side. Encourage the children to identify which words fit which pictures and stick them underneath the appropriate picture. Glue the title and 'The end' to the reverse side.

Element C24.3 Help develop children's writing skills

➤ **C24.3**: *range 1a,* · · · Your assessor can observe and question you. ◄
b, 2c, 4c

Label it!

Number of children: individual children or small groups.

Resources

Card; thick felt pens; scissors or guillotine; sticky notes; hook and loop fastenings; Blu-Tack; laminator if available.

Preparation

Prepare some labels yourself and some with the children.

What to do

➤ Use children's individual name labels for recognition.

➤ Label shelves, drawers and boxes to aid sorting equipment and tidying up.

➤ Make door signs for general information or to personalise requests and instructions, such as, 'Welcome', 'Class 1', 'Keep out' and 'Please knock'.

➤ Children for whom English is a second language will find labels useful for seeing as well as hearing words they may be just learning.

➤ Label objects in the role-play area. For example, a 'Hairdresser's' will have 'shampoo', 'brush', 'mirror', 'comb', 'magazines' and 'towels'.

➤ Attach hook and loop fastenings to the backs of cards to make a changeable display for the days of the week or weather identification.

➤ Make labels for the fridge, describing the contents. Attach with magnets.

Support and extension

Encourage experienced children to produce their own labels. Invite less skilled children to read and place labels you have made.

✔ **Tip**

➤ Use play dough to make letter shapes.

C24.3: 1

Evaluation

Did the children gain confidence in their reading and writing skills using only one- or two-word labels? Can you think of other ways of using labels, signs and captions? Can you make any suggestions for using labels to parents?

Supporting activity

➤ Make instruction cards, such as recipes, the order to pack an activity away, contents listings, games instructions and outlining the routine. ◄ · · **C24.3**: 1, 2, 3, 4, 5, 6, 8, 9, 10

Case study

➤ Sadie's parents have enrolled her at your setting as it offers a caring environment and had a good OFSTED report. However, they are anxious, as a local nursery produces lots of worksheets and they wonder why their friend's children are reading and writing while Sadie is just playing. How can you reassure them and what examples of reading, pre-writing and early reading skills can you show them? Write down the case study with your responses for your portfolio.

C24.3: 1, 2 ◄

Follow on

➤ Write simple words on cards in languages other than English, with the English word underneath. You can also include a phonetic spelling. Display and show the children that words can be written and spoken in different ways.

Cross-reference to ◄ **C11**

Questions

(See answer pointers at end of chapter.)

➤ **7.** *What forms of stimulation can you suggest to encourage a child to write?* · · **C24.3**: 3 ◄

➤ **8.** *Describe some writing forms and the characteristics that define them.* · · · · **C24.3**: 6 ◄

➤ **9.** *What factors are significant for children in order to develop competent* · · · · **C24.3**: 7 ◄
writing skills?

Record the questions and your full answers and share these with your assessor.

Did you know?

About ten per cent of children are left-handed. This can make it more difficult for them to write, as their writing hand tends to cover up the words. Encourage the child to hold the pencil further up, to position the paper at an angle to the body and to use a pencil grip to speed up the process.

Extra idea

➤ **C24.3**: 3 · · · · · · · Use the 'Fill the gaps' photocopiable sheet on page 158 to encourage ◄ children to write the appropriate word in the gaps.

Practical ways of collecting evidence

As reading and writing at Key Stage 1 is a substantial learning area it should not be difficult to find opportunities to be directly observed by your assessor. To raise your awareness of when reading and writing takes place, keep a diary for a few days. Note when you listen to children read, read a story, read instructions, supervise writing practice, observe spontaneous mark-making, read notices together and other similar activities. Include in your portfolio.

Check your progress

For this Unit you are expected to be directly observed for at least one aspect of the range statements for each of the three Elements. If some of the performance criteria have not been observed then you will need to present other types of evidence, such as reflective accounts of work, plans and preparation for reading and writing activities, witness testimonies, diary entries and work products such as progress records.

Answer pointers

Ensure your answers are fully made for your assessor.

1. Without distraction. Position. Sitting by adult. Comfortable. Book in front of them. Left to right. Top to bottom. Punctuation.
2. Pictures. Context. Re-reading. Sounding out words. Remind children.
3. Letter shapes. Spaces. Capitals. Lower case. Sounds. Words. Sentences.
4. Records. Teacher. Curriculum. Learning plans. Previous experience.
5. Personal interests. Stimulate imagination. Pleasurable. Useful. Appropriate.
6. Choice. Library. Reward. Set tasks. Selection for home link.
7. Stories. Access to materials. Poems. Experience. Activities in the setting.
8. Narratives. Poems. Non-fiction. Fiction. Lists. Messages. Records. Factual. Short. Imagination. Beginning, middle and end.
9. Script. Lower case. Left to right. Spaces. Spelling. Punctuation. Capitals.

Further information

How to Teach Your Child to Read from 2 Years Old by Bill Gillham (Ward Lock, 1998)

C25 Support the development of children's mathematical skills

This Unit focuses on supporting teachers to implement mathematics skills. It covers the use and application of mathematics, understanding number and the use of shape, space and measurement. It is appropriate for practitioners in all settings where children are supported individually or in groups, especially those supporting teachers at Key Stage 1 or its equivalent.

This chapter will enable you to:
C25.1 Help children to use and apply mathematics
C25.2 Support children's understanding and use of number
C25.3 Help children develop their understanding and use of shape, space and measures.

Element C25.1 Help children to use and apply mathematics

➤ Your assessor can observe and question you.· **C25.1**: *range 1a, b, 2a, 3c* ◀

Maths in the kitchen
Number of children: small groups.

Resources
40g plain flour; 40g cornflour; 20g cocoa; 20g icing sugar; 80g soft margarine; decorations such as icing sugar, water, lemon juice, glacé cherries, chocolate spread, sugar strands or icing flowers; mixing bowl; wooden spoon; non-stick baking tray; large spoon; teaspoon; plate; kitchen scales; palette knife; sieve.

Preparation
Plan the activity using the 'Activity plan' photocopiable sheet on page 131. Check for allergies or dietary requirements. Clean surfaces, wash your hands and wear a clean apron. Heat the oven to 375°F/190°C/Gas Mark 5.

What to do
➤ Ask the children to wash their hands and put on clean aprons.
➤ Discuss sets, such as two spoons, a bowl and a baking tray.
➤ Encourage the children to identify the shapes, such as the circular rim of the bowl, the rectangular baking tray and the cylindrical cocoa tin.
➤ Let the children weigh out the ingredients.
➤ Help the children sieve the flour, cornflour, sugar and cocoa into the bowl.

 Tip

➤ Sorting small objects encourages children to think of groupings.

C25.1: 3

➤ Take every opportunity to use mathematical language in describing routine tasks.

C25.1: 6

Encourage children to explain their reasons for the way they do things, to test ideas, evaluate and interpret information.

C25.1: 7

➤ Add the margarine and mix thoroughly until a ball of dough is formed.
➤ Let the children roll teaspoonfuls of dough into 20 balls and press down gently on the baking tray. Leave space between the biscuits to spread.
➤ Bake for 20 minutes and cool before removing from the baking tray.
➤ Let the children count the biscuits and then choose how they would like to decorate them.

Support and extension
Help younger children where necessary. Challenge older children to write out their own recipe sheet.

Evaluation
How many different learning opportunities were there? Were you able to apply mathematical language and concepts to activities in the kitchen? How can you make it more challenging in the future?

Supporting activity

➤ *C24.1: 1, 2, 3, 6,* · · ·
10

Plan a tea party with the children. Outline and plan the event. Make a 'things ◄ to do list'. Encourage the children to write out some simple recipes (number and sequence), shop for the ingredients they will need (number and money), write out menus (order), make table decorations (measurement, symmetry and pattern), cook the food (weight, counting and temperature) and set out the chairs and cutlery (counting, pairing and sets). Record the children's progress.

Case study

➤ *C25.1: 3, 8* · · · · · ·

Catrina lives with her mum and little sister on a remote estate. Her mum ◄ can only get to the setting occasionally and is worried that Catrina will miss out on her education because she cannot help her. She is particularly anxious about mathematics. How can you encourage and reassure her that there are lots of everyday opportunities for Catrina to get a good grounding in the subject? Write down the case study with your responses for your portfolio.

Follow on

➤ *C25.1: 6, cross-* · · · ·
reference to **P2**

Prepare maths games and activities for parents to use at home with their ◄ children. Suggest that the parents try them out and give you feedback.

Questions
(See answer pointers at end of chapter.)

➤ *C25.1: 3* · · · · · · · · **1.** *Suggest ways to carry out practical mathematical tasks in the setting.* ◄
➤ *C25.1: 4* · · · · · · · · **2.** *What mathematical equipment can you expect to see in the setting?* ◄
➤ *C25.1: 6* · · · · · · · · **3.** *Give examples of mathematical language used in the early years.* ◄

Record the questions and your full answers and share these with your assessor.

Did you know?
'Mathematical development depends on becoming confident and competent in learning and using key skills.' *Curriculum Guidance for the Foundation Stage* (DfEE, 2000)

Extra idea
➤ Use potato prints in two colours for making a pattern sequence. · · · · · · · · **C25.1**: 9 ◄

Element C25.2 Support children's understanding and use of number

➤ Your assessor can observe and question you. · · · · · · · · · · · · · **C25.2**: *range 1a, b,* ◄
2a, b, c, 3a, b, c

Caterpillar frieze
Number of children: small groups.

Resources
21 squares of coloured paper, approximately 20cm x 20cm; 20 pieces of thin card, 10cm x 10cm; Blu-Tack; felt-tipped pens; plate; scissors; staple gun; display board; books and posters showing butterflies and caterpillars.

Preparation
Plan the activity using the 'Activity plan' photocopiable sheet on page 131. Cut out the numerals 1 to 20 from the thin card.

What to do
➤ Show the children the books and talk about patterns in nature.
➤ Ask the children to draw around the plate and cut out to make a circle. Invite them to cover the circle with small repeat patterns, using felt-tipped pens, based on the natural designs discussed.
➤ When the children have finished, make one circle into a caterpillar's head.
➤ Fix a numeral in the centre of each circle with Blu-tack.
➤ Ask the children to arrange the circles in numerical order.
➤ Make simple number patterns by removing every second or third number.
➤ Use the caterpillar as a number line and give each child a number to find.

Support and extension
Help younger children to create simple number patterns. Challenge older children to create their own number patterns.

Evaluation
How else can you use the frieze? Did you get the result you anticipated? Were the children able to predict the patterns? Were there any surprises?

Supporting activity
Collect number worksheets in a file for future reference. If you have bought a book, you may have the right to copy pages. It will say in the book.

Tip
➤ Give motivation stickers to encourage the children.

C25.2: 8

➤ Display the setting's telephone number in the imaginative play area beside the telephone and a telephone directory for 'checking' numbers.

C25.2: 3, 5

➤ **C25.2**: *2, 5, 6* · · · ·

Case study
Zahra is confident with numbers but has difficulty calculating fractions. You want to try different practical methods to help her to grasp the concept. Suggest ways to help her understand and, then, move from the visual practical approach to the abstract. Write down the case study with your responses for your portfolio. ◀

➤ **C25.2**: *1, 6* · · · · · ·

Follow on
Think about coins as part of a whole and the activities you can do using play money, coin ink stampers, rubbings or coins of the children's own creation. ◀

Questions
(See answer pointers at end of chapter.)

➤ **C25.2**: *4* · · · · · · ·   **4.** *What sort of support do children need to effectively record number work?* ◀

➤ **C25.2**: *7* · · · · · · ·   **5.** *How can you help children understand number and computation?* ◀

➤ **C25.2**: *9* · · · · · · ·   **6.** *How will you deal with a child who has difficulties understanding numbers.* ◀

Record the questions and your full answers and share these with your assessor.

Did you know?
Young children need to learn a mathematical language suitable to their developmental level. Keep it simple and use words like 'more', 'less', 'odd', 'even', 'add' and 'addition', 'subtraction' and 'take away', 'pair' and 'double'.

Extra idea

➤ **C25.2**: *1, 3, 4, 5,* · · ·   Use the 'Up the garden path' photocopiable sheet on page 159. As a group, ◀
6, 7, 8, 9   say the numbers, count the spaces, follow instructions and write the scores.

Element C25.3 Help children develop their understanding and use of shape, space and measures

➤ **C25.3**: *range 1a, b* · ·   Your assessor can observe and question you. ◀

Shapes and boxes
Number of children: small groups.

Resources
Resources appropriate to the chosen activity.

Preparation
Plan the activity using the 'Activity plan' photocopiable sheet on page 131. Prepare any resources.

What to do

➤ Set the imaginative play area up as a supermarket, with empty packets and containers. Let the children identify the shapes that they can see, such as cubes, cones and prisms.

➤ Offer shaped packets, tubes and card and encourage the children to build 3-D models.

➤ Discuss different sizes using traditional Russian nesting dolls.

➤ Play 'Spot the shape' with items from around the room.

➤ Ask the children to sort cardboard shapes, by their different qualities, such as 'all curved surfaces', 'three sides', 'two faces' or 'four corners'.

➤ Invite the children to print shapes using different-shaped potato cuts.

✓ Tip

➤ Give the children ribbons to whirl in PE sessions, to give a physical experience of shape. Ask them to describe the actions, movement and form.

C25.3: 5

Support and extension

Base the activities on the developmental level of the children. Help those having difficulties and present greater challenges for those who are able.

Evaluation

Did you maintain the children's interest and understanding with these activities? Were the activities successful? How can they be improved? Did you create your own ideas? Did you record the children's progress?

Supporting activity

➤ Write a reflective account of your participation and how the children responded, how you dealt with difficulties and how you encouraged the children. Place in your portfolio.

C25.3: 5, 10, 11, ◄
cross-reference to **C5**,
C7

Case study

➤ Jake has special educational needs and boundless energy. To keep his interest there has to be movement in the activity. You have a large hall and an outdoor play area in the setting. Suggest activities to satisfy Jake's need for action as well as teaching him about shapes and recognising quarter and half turns? Write down the case study with your responses for your portfolio.

C25.3: 1, 2, 3, 5, 6, 9 ◄

Follow on

➤ Make your own list of activities to cover time, measurement and capacity. When you think of an idea for an activity make a note of it for the future.

C25.3: 7 ◄

Questions

(See answer pointers at end of chapter.)

➤ **7.** *Children moving on from Reception will bring play-oriented experiences with them into Year One. Can you identify those that develop mathematical concepts?*

C25.3: 1 ◄

➤ **8.** *How can IT be used to aid the understanding of shape, space and measures?*

C25.3: 4 ◄

➤ **9.** *Identify the standard and non-standard instruments of measurement you can expect to see in an early years setting and describe how you use them.*

C25.3: 7 ◄

Record the questions and your full answers and share these with your assessor.

Did you know?

The mathematical language for a:

➤ Pattern: an arrangement of numbers, shapes or colours.

➤ Sphere: a solid figure bounded by a surface of which all points are the same distance from the centre.

➤ Spiral: a curve that moves out from a central point.

➤ Symmetry: shapes and patterns with matching halves, one reflecting the other.

➤ Tessellate: shapes fitting snugly together without spaces between them.

➤ Triangle: a shape with three angles and three sides.

Extra idea

➤ **C25.3**: 3, 4, 6 · · · · · Copy the 'Shape matching' photocopiable sheet on page 160 and use with ◄ the children to aid recognition of 2-D mathematical shapes.

Practical ways of collecting evidence

Keep a logbook to record all the mathematical activities you identify over a few days. This will include the time identified as numeracy or maths time, as well as the spontaneous opportunities in play, PE, crafts and other activities.

Check your progress

Your assessor will need to directly observe at least one aspect of each of the range statements. Other methods to gain evidence include inspecting the setting in relation to your responsibility in supporting the teacher, reflective accounts, diaries, plans and witness testimonies.

Answer pointers

Ensure your answers are fully made for your assessor.

1. Counting. Estimating. Balancing. Comparing. Fitting together.

2. Balance scales. Dice. Clocks. Calculator. Blocks. Measuring sticks.

3. Addition. Subtraction. Half. Quarter. First. Last. More than. Less than. Pattern. Rectangle. Cube.

4. Exposure. Practice. Praise. Printouts. Small groups. Self-esteem.

5. Practical application. Patience. Games. Practice. Use experiences. Repeat.

6. Build confidence. Not undermine. Praise. Build on what they know. Repeat.

7. Water. Sand. Play dough. Mass. Capacity. Modelling. Fractions. Weight.

8. Computer programs. Moving programmable robots. Clocks. Scales.

9. Metre stick. Scales. Ruler. Containers. Clocks. Feet. String. Estimate. Tape measure. Measuring jug. Height chart.

Further information

One, Two, Skip a Few! Illustrated by Roberta Arenson, First Number Rhymes series (Barefoot Books, 1999)

Mathematical Development by Jenni Tavener, Goals for the Foundation Stage series (Scholastic, 2002)

Activity plan

Who is it for?	Resources:
Preparation:	**Why? (Areas of Learning)**

Activity: _____

Your part:	Evaluation:
Support and extension:	
	Comment:

Name: _____ Date: _____ Witness: _____

Spider chart

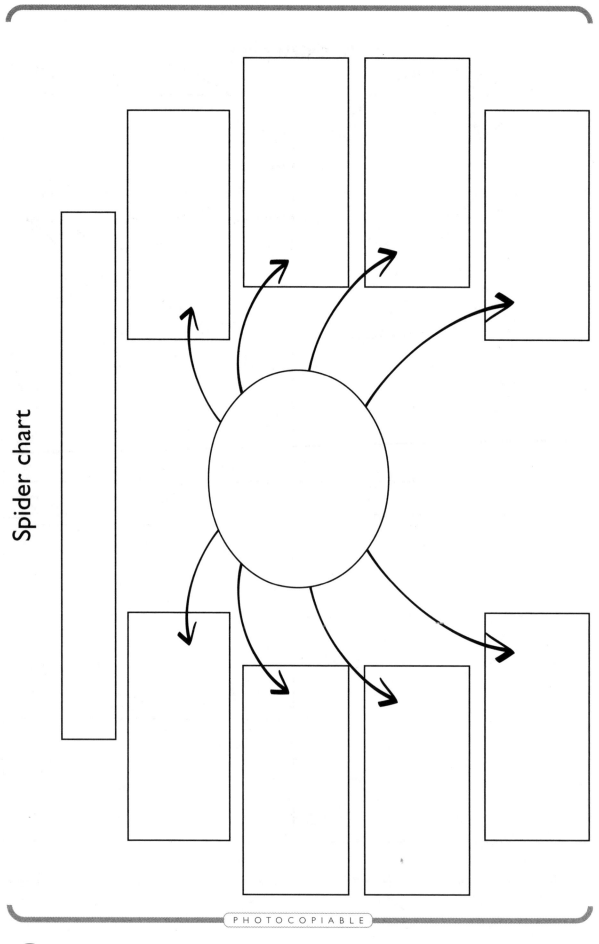

I can:

Name: Date:

early years training & management   Gaining your NVQ Level 3 in Early Years Care and Education   ■SCHOLASTIC   133

Mendhi

SCHOLASTIC   Gaining your NVQ Level 3 in Early Years Care and Education   early years training & management

Housey housey

Semi-detached house

Travellers wagon

Block of flats

Bungalow

Terraced house

Detached house

House boat

Thatched cottage

Religious and cultural designs

Founding of the Khalsa movement
Baisakhi

Sikh

Confucianism

Make sweets to give as a present
Eid-ul-Fitr

Islam

Lotus flower

The orange represents the world, the red ribbon is the blood of Christ, the fruit and nuts are the fruits of the earth and the candle is Christ, the light of the world
Christingle
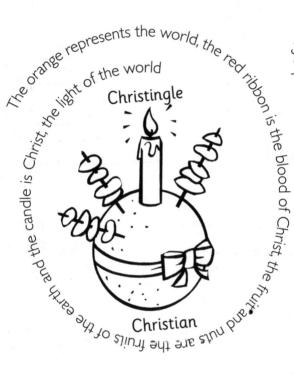
Christian

Spring festival of joy. Use powder paint to make displays
Holi

Hindu

Eggs represent new life
Easter

Christian

Judaism

Festivals of light
Divali

Hindu
Diva

Tell the Christmas story
Christmas

Christian

Menorah

Hanukkah
Jewish

■SCHOLASTIC   Gaining your NVQ Level 3 in Early Years Care and Education   early years training & management

Play dough recipes

1 Golden gloss

3 cups plain flour
1 cup salt
1 tablespoon cooking oil
Yellow or orange colouring (food colouring or powder paint)
Water as required

Mix ingredients together and knead until smooth and glossy. No cooking is required. This is a smooth, tough dough with a nice gleam that holds its shape, is good for modelling, is easily cut with cutters, is pliable and pleasant to handle.

2 Fridge dough

2 cups plain flour
1 cup salt
Colouring (food colouring or powder paint)
Water as required

Mix ingredients together and knead until smooth and glossy. No cooking is required. The salt content helps preserve the dough. This dough is good for modelling, retains its shape and handles well. It will keep for two weeks if stored in a plastic box or bag in the fridge. Add extra water to use the mixture as finger-paint.

3 Cooked play dough

2 cups plain flour
1 cup salt
2 cups water
2 tablespoons cooking oil
2 teaspoons cream of tartar
1 dessertspoon powder paint or a small amount of food colouring

Place all the ingredients in a saucepan and cook over a medium heat. Stir constantly to prevent sticking. Remove from the heat when the mixture comes away from the side of the saucepan. Knead the dough well and store in an airtight container. This dough is long lasting and similar to commercially-produced dough. It is pleasant to handle, pliable and has good modelling qualities.

Reward chart

Name: _____

Date	Monday	Tuesday	Wednesday	Thursday	Friday	Saturday	Sunday

All in good time

It is all right to **push**

It is all right to **bite**

It is all right to **fight**

It is all right to **be kind**

It is all right to **hit**

It is all right to **share**

It is all right to **be unkind**

It is all right to **wait for your turn**

It is all right to **be friends**

It is all right to **smile**

PHOTOCOPIABLE

Recipes

Savoury scones

225g self-raising flour
50g soft butter
50g grated Cheddar cheese
120ml milk
Pinch of salt

- Rub the butter, salt and flour together until the mixture resembles breadcrumbs.

- Mix the cheese in and add the milk slowly, stirring together.

- Knead the mixture until it forms a stiff dough and then roll out to 2cm thickness, adding flour to the surface and rolling-pin to stop the dough sticking.

- Cut circles out of the dough with pastry cutters.

- Brush the top of the scones with milk and sprinkle with a little cheese.

- Bake in the oven for 12 to 15 minutes at 425°F/220°C/Gas Mark 7.

Cheese fingers

350g ready-made puff pastry
50g grated Cheddar cheese
1 egg

- Roll the pastry into a rectangle, approximately 25cm by 20cm.

- Beat the egg and brush over the pastry.

- Sprinkle cheese over half the pastry.

- Fold the pastry over and roll it flat again.

- Brush the top with egg and cut into fingers.

- Place the fingers on a baking tray and bake in the oven for ten minutes at 425°F/ 220°C/Gas Mark 7.

Shortbread

175g plain flour
50g caster sugar
125g soft butter
1 tablespoon milk

- Rub the flour, sugar and butter together until the mixture resembles breadcrumbs.

- Add the milk and mix together with your hands until the mixture forms a soft dough.

- Roll the dough flat and cut into shapes with pastry cutters.

- Brush the top of the biscuits with milk and sprinkle with a little sugar.

- Bake in the oven for 15 to 20 minutes at 425°F/220°C/Gas Mark 7.

Bread rolls

350g strong flour
3g dried yeast
Pinch of salt
1 dessertspoon sunflower oil
210ml warm water

- Put the dry ingredients into a bowl.

- Add the oil and water and mix together, adding extra flour if the dough is too sticky.

- Knead the dough.

- Divide the dough into small balls and place on the baking tray in a warm place until the balls have doubled in size.

- Bake in the oven for 15 to 20 minutes at 450°F/230°C/Gas Mark 8.

Rangoli patterns

Development chart

Name: _____

Dates from: _____

To: _____

Recorded by: _____

Picture sequence

Body popping

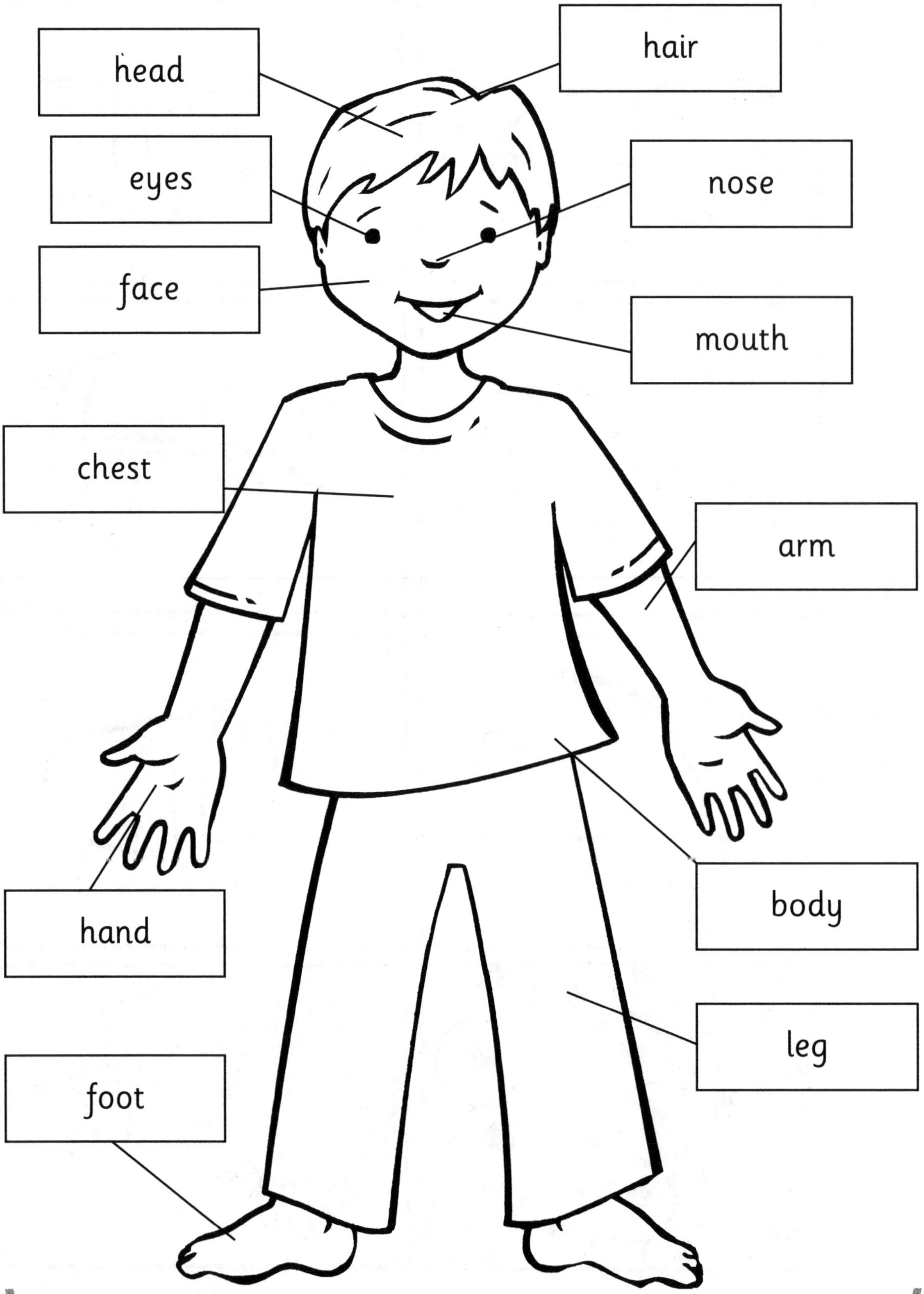

head

hair

eyes

nose

face

mouth

chest

arm

hand

body

foot

leg

Safety game

No sweets from a stranger

Tell someone you trust

Your body is yours

Stay with your friends

Do not get into a stranger's car

If frightened, shout and run

Do not keep bad secrets

Always tell your parents where you are going

If you do not like it, say, 'NO'

Observation tick chart

Child(ren): _____ _____ Age(s): _____									

Date: _____   Observation time scale: _____

Subject: _____

Observer: _____

  SCHOLASTIC   Gaining your NVQ Level 3 in Early Years Care and Education   *early years* **training & management**

Event sampling chart

Time	Activity	Who with	Language	Comment

Date: _____

Identification of child: _____ Age: _____

Researcher: _____

Accident game

What if…

What if…	What if…
We ring 999?	We see a fire?
What if…	What if…
We bump our knee?	We break our arm?
What if…	What if…
Our tummy hurts?	We bang our head?
What if…	What if…
We see the doctor?	We see a sharp knife?
What if…	What if…
We burn ourselves?	We hear the fire alarm?

the iron burns us, what do we do? …

we bump our head, where do we go for help? …

we make a 999 call, who will come? …

our tummy hurts, what do we tell the carer? …

there is a fire, what do we have to do? …

Design a play area

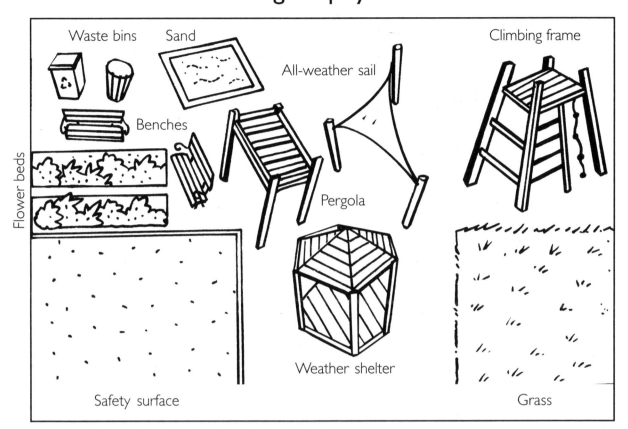

Waste bins   Sand

All-weather sail

Climbing frame

Benches

Flower beds

Pergola

Weather shelter

Safety surface

Grass

Safe play area

Long-term planning

Date from: _____ to: _____

Theme	Jan	Feb	Mar	Apr	May	Jun	Jul	Aug	Sep	Oct	Nov	Dec
Special events												
Personal, social and emotional development												
Communication, language and literacy												
Mathematical development												
Knowledge and understanding of the world												
Physical development												
Creative development												
Notes												

Enlarge sheet to A3.

Medium-term planning

Date from: _____ to: _____

Months					
Theme					
Personal, social and emotional development					
Communication, language and literacy					
Mathematical development					
Knowledge and understanding of the world					
Physical development					
Creative development					

Enlarge sheet to A3 if required.

Short-term planning

Week beginning: _____

Theme	Monday	Tuesday	Wednesday	Thursday	Friday
Personal, social and emotional development					
Communication, language and literacy					
Mathematical development					
Knowledge and understanding of the world					
Physical development					
Creative development					

Topic web

Topic	
Personal, social and emotional development	Communication, language and literacy
Mathematical development	Knowledge and understanding of the world
Physical development	Creative development

Parental action plan

Child's name:
Parent contacted: Date:
Contact at setting:
Concern or information exchange:
Date meeting arranged:
Location:
Notes on meeting:
Action by parent:
Action by setting:
Date of review:
Notes:

Baby development and stimulation chart

Child's name: _____ Date: _____

Gross motor skills:	Fine motor skills:
Social and emotional development:	Cognitive:
Communication:	Age and stage appropriate stimulation:

Describe what the baby can do in the appropriate boxes.
Suggest games, play and stimulating activities to aid development.

Menu sheet

	Monday	Tuesday	Wednesday	Thursday	Friday
Breakfast					
Lunch					
Tea					
Additional snacks or drinks					

Date: _____

The story of the snowman

The end.	Put one on top of the other.	My snowman story by _____
We are making snowballs.	Look at our snowman.	Look at the snow falling.

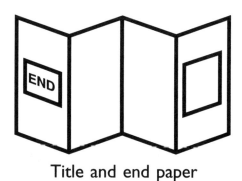

Title and end paper

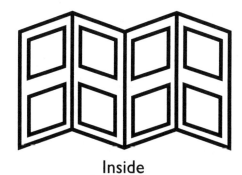

Inside

Fill the gaps

Rock-a-bye _ _ _ _ _
on the _ _ _ _ top,
When the _ _ _ _ blows
the cradle will _ _ _ _.
When _ _ _ bough breaks
the cradle _ _ _ _ fall,
Down will come _ _ _ _
cradle _ _ _ all.

Fill in these missing words:

wind   tree   rock

will   baby   and   the   baby

PHOTOCOPIABLE

SCHOLASTIC   Gaining your NVQ Level 3 in Early Years Care and Education   early years **training & management**

Up the garden path

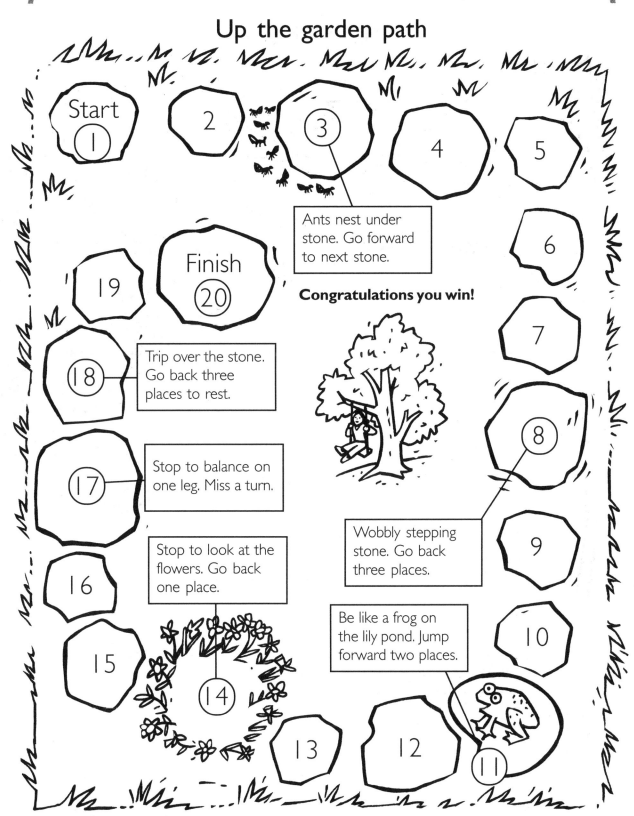

Start 1

2

3 — Ants nest under stone. Go forward to next stone.

4

5

6

7

Congratulations you win!

8 — Wobbly stepping stone. Go back three places.

9

10

11 — Be like a frog on the lily pond. Jump forward two places.

12

13

14 — Stop to look at the flowers. Go back one place.

15

16

17 — Stop to balance on one leg. Miss a turn.

18 — Trip over the stone. Go back three places to rest.

19

Finish 20

This is a game for two to four players. Use small pebbles for counters. Throw a dice in turns and move round the stepping stones. Follow the instructions along the way. The winner is the first to reach 20.

PHOTOCOPIABLE

Shape matching

Name: _____

Draw a line to match the shapes up.

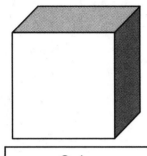

Cube

Cylinder

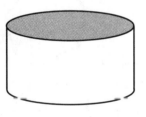

Cylinder

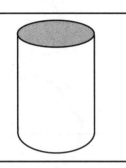

Cone

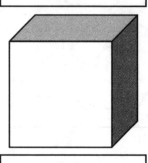

Cylinder

Cube

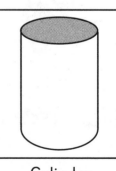

Cone

Cylinder

■SCHOLASTIC   Gaining your NVQ Level 3 in Early Years Care and Education   early years training & management